Hotel and Catering Accounts

Hotel and Catering Accounts

R. D. Boardman, FCA

Butterworth-Heinemann Ltd
Halley Court, Jordan Hill, Oxford OX2 8EJ

Ⓡ A member of the Reed Elsevier group

OXFORD LONDON BOSTON
MUNICH NEW DELHI SINGAPORE SYDNEY
TOKYO TORONTO WELLINGTON

First published 1991
Reprinted 1994

British Library Cataloguing in Publication Data
Boardman, R. D.
    Hotel and catering accounts.
    1. Catering. Management
    I. Title
    647.95068

ISBN 0 7506 0086 1

Set by Cambridge Composing (UK) Ltd, Cambridge
Printed and bound in Great Britain by
M & A Thomson Litho Ltd, East Kilbride, Scotland.

Contents

Preface

An understanding of accounts and cost statements is vital to hotel and catering management, but textbooks written by accountants for accountants are not always readily translated into a catering relevance. Accounting is no different from other disciplines in having its own jargon, and where this helps to establish a precise meaning, it is very useful, so long as the meaning is clear.

I have written this book with caterers and catering students in mind, and have tried to avoid using jargon without at least first explaining it. Illustrations have been given in the form of typical examination type questions followed by answers, and students may find it useful to tackle each question themselves before going on to read the answer.

It is hoped that this one book will cover the range of accounts, costing, and budgeting necessary to caterers. In trying to achieve this I have given consideration to hotel and catering management examinations, without over-emphasis on aspects which are not related to hotel and catering management.

R. D. Boardman

1 Introduction to accounting

Book-keeping and accounting arise from the need to know whether an enterprise is financially successful or not. They record in a systematic way all the activities of the enterprise so far as they can be expressed in terms of money.

If a business is to avoid falling into financial difficulty, the people concerned with its management must have constant information about the financial effect of its operations. All transactions to do with money or money's worth, i.e. a service or commodity capable of being expressed in terms of money, need to be recorded systematically, and from these records summaries should be prepared to show what degree of profitability has been achieved, and what is the current financial state of affairs. *Book-keeping* is the term for the system used for writing up the financial records, and *accounting* is the preparation of statements of financial summaries from those records. Other terms which may be defined now in order to avoid confusion are *auditing*, which means verifying and reporting on the accounting performed by someone else, and *accountancy*, which is a more general term denoting the practice of dealing with these and other related matters such as taxation.

Some information would be available to us if we just made a note of each transaction as it occurred, in the form of a diary, but this would not show us the cumulative effect of all our transactions. It would be difficult to ascertain the *totals* of income and expenses, the balance of cash available, or debts owing. In order to record our financial transactions properly it is necessary first to recognise the nature of a transaction, which always has a twofold aspect. Since the transaction consists of money or money's worth moving from one person to another, it follows that it comprises both a giving and a receiving. Both aspects must be recorded if our records are to be complete. If we pay a creditor (a person to whom money is owed) the £10 we owe him, we must record the fact that we have given out £10 (our cash resources are now £10 less) *and* that he has received £10 (the debt due to him is now £10 less). Without either of these records our information would be incomplete, and we would be left uncertain about the amount of our cash or the amount of our debts.

The system of recording financial transactions which has been used throughout the world since the Middle Ages is known as *double-entry book-keeping*, because it calls for two entries to be made in respect of each transaction, one entry for each of the two aspects. Both entries may be made as single items, or more likely the entry for one aspect will be made by a single item while the entry for the other aspect is included in a list, but two entries there must be. The correctness of the concept is demonstrated by the fact that it has remained valid despite all the changes in trade and methods of recording over the centuries. The appearance of book-keeping has changed with the advent of computers, and the double-entry effect may be encompassed by the programme used, instead of needing to hit the same keys twice, but the underlying principles have not changed. For the time being we shall ignore computers and concentrate on the principles as they would be followed in handwritten books of account.

The two aspects of each transaction can be summarised under a total of six headings which can conveniently be grouped in pairs:

Assets	Liabilities
Expenses	Income
Losses	Profits

The headings listed on the left are similar in nature, while those on the right are their opposites. It may seem surprising to refer to assets and expenses as similar in nature, until you consider that they both have to be paid for. The only difference is the lasting quality of the asset over a period of time, whereas the amount paid for the expense is gone.

An *asset* is something we own, such as furniture, stock-in-trade, cash or a debt due to us. Of these four examples the first three are tangible objects, but a debt due to us is just as much something we own, even though it is intangible. We own the right to collect a sum of money, and it is possible to sell that right to someone else.

A *liability* is an amount which we owe to someone else, and thus may be regarded as the opposite of an asset. This is one of those words which have been adopted by the public for popular use in a different sense – 'The goalkeeper is more of a liability to the side than an asset' uses words with an obvious book-keeping origin, but not in their proper meaning. We shall always use the words assets and liabilities to mean ownership and indebtedness to others.

Income denotes sums receivable without an increase in liabilities, thus causing an increase in total wealth. The earnings from trade, from the provision of services, or interest on money invested, are all income producing an increase in wealth. A loan received, on the other hand, is not income because it creates a new liability, and so does not increase our wealth.

Expenses are sums expended in earning the income, for which no lasting asset has been received in exchange, and total wealth has therefore been reduced. Such items as rent, rates, wages to staff, gas and electricity charges are expenses.

Profits are the result when income is greater than expenses, so that capital (the wealth used in a business) is increased.

Losses are the result when expenses are greater than income, so there is a loss of capital.

Each of the two aspects of every transaction will consist of an increase or reduction under one of these headings. You will see that the headings have been set out in one list of three on the left, and one list of three opposites on the right. If the two aspects of a transaction are concerned with two headings on the same side, then the effect will be to increase one and reduce the other. If they concern headings on opposite sides, then the effect will be to reduce both or to increase both. We have already seen that paying a creditor the £10 we owed him made our cash resources £10 less (reduction of an asset) and made the debt due to the creditor £10 less (reduction of a liability). The headings assets and liabilities are on opposite sides, so both were reduced. All other transactions may be analysed into two aspects as in the following examples:

Transaction	*Aspect 1*	*Aspect 2*
Purchase of goods for cash	Expense (cost of goods sold) increased	Asset (cash) reduced

Expenses and assets are on the same side, so if one is increased, the other is reduced.

Transaction	*Aspect 1*	*Aspect 2*
Purchase of goods on credit	Expense (cost of goods sold) increased	Liability (creditor) increased

The two aspects are expenses and liabilities, and both are increased. Note that the effect on the expense is the same as in the previous example. It makes no difference to the expense whether the transaction was for cash or on credit, the expense has still been increased. The difference between the two transactions is in the other aspect – the reduction of cash or the increase in liabilities.

Transaction	*Aspect 1*	*Aspect 2*
Office typewriter bought on credit	Asset (office equipment) increased	Liability (creditor) increased

Assets and liabilities are both increased.

Transaction	*Aspect 1*	*Aspect 2*
Motor van bought by cheque	Asset (motor vans) increased	Asset (bank balance) reduced

One asset is increased, and another asset reduced.

Transaction	*Aspect 1*	*Aspect 2*
Cash received from debtor	Asset (cash) increased	Asset (debtors) reduced

A debtor is a person who owes money, in this case to us, so the debt was one of our assets. It has now been exchanged for another asset (cash).

Transaction	*Aspect 1*	*Aspect 2*
Goods sold on credit	Asset (debtors) increased	Income (sales) increased

Double-entry book-keeping requires all these matters to be entered in a ledger, where items of a similar sort can be listed together, to be summarised later. The entries will be debit entries (those on the left-hand side of a handwritten ledger page) or credit entries (those on the right-hand side), and the dual aspect of each transaction will cause a double entry in the ledger, one debit and one credit of equal amounts.

Note that in our ledger the terms are used in the way that they relate to us. A debtor is someone who owes money to us. If a debt is owing at all, then one party must be a debtor and the other party must be a creditor, but we record it as it affects us. If the bank sends us a statement saying we have a credit balance in our account in their books, they mean that we are their creditors. They are holding some of our money which they owe to us. It follows that they are our debtors, and would be shown as such, i.e. a debit balance, in our books. If the account is overdrawn of course, the roles are reversed, and we are shown as debtors in their books, while they are creditors in ours.

The result of making a double entry for every transaction is that the entries in the ledger after a period of time consist of very many debits and very many credits of the same amount, all grouped under headings of different kinds of assets, liabilities, expenses, and income, so that the totals of each kind of heading are shown. The totals of each kind of debit item will not be the same as each kind of credit item, but the total of all debit items will be the same as the total of all credit items. Periodically a list of these amounts will be prepared, called a trial balance, from which accounting statements can be prepared. An example is given below:

EXCEL RESTAURANT

Trial balance as at 31 October 19..

	Debit (Dr) £	Credit (Cr) £
Sales		74,200
Cost of goods sold	26,700	
Wages and salaries	18,200	
Other expenses	19,700	
Premises	80,000	
Furniture and equipment	30,000	
China and glass	4,000	
Stock in hand	2,000	
Debtors	1,000	
Creditors		6,000
Bank balance	6,800	
Cash in hand	200	
Proprietor's capital at beginning of year		58,400
Loan from Merchant Bank PLC		50,000
	188,600	188,600

It will be seen that the debit items are all assets or expenses, while the credit items are income or liabilities. Since the figures relate to the business rather than the proprietor himself, the capital is a liability of the business owing to the proprietor. The amounts of income and expenses constitute the information necessary to decide whether the business has made a profit or a loss during the period just ended. The assets and liabilities also shown on the trial balance at the end of that period show the wealth of the business after its period of trading activities. These two matters can be shown in accounting statements called respectively 'profit and loss account' and 'balance sheet', the first being for a period of time, usually a year, and the second being as at a given date at the end of that period. See the following examples:

EXCEL RESTAURANT
Profit and loss account for the year ended 31 October 19..

	£	£
Sales		74,200
Less expenses:		
Cost of goods sold	26,700	
Wages and salaries	18,200	
Other expenses	19,700	
		64,600
Net profit for the year		9,600

The net profit represents an increase in the wealth of the business belonging to the proprietor, and this will be reflected in the amount of his capital shown in the balance sheet.

EXCEL RESTAURANT
Balance sheet as at 31 October 19..

Assets	£	£
Premises		80,000
Furniture and equipment		30,000
China and glass		4,000
Stocks of food and wine		2,000
Debtors		1,000
Cash at bank and in hand		7,000
		124,000
Less liabilities due for imminent payment		6,000
		118,000
Financed by:		
Proprietor's capital as last year	58,400	
Add net profit to date	9,600	
		68,000
Borrowed capital		50,000
		118,000

The way in which this information is presented may vary from one balance sheet to another, just as a verbal account of facts by different people would be presented differently, but the basic form will be the same. It is customary now to show the two parts of the statement one under the other, whereas they used to be shown side by side. The liabilities used to be shown in the same part as the capital, whereas now they are usually deducted from the assets. The difference is not one of principle but of presentation, which is constantly developing in an effort to improve the understanding of the information given. Balance Sheets will be dealt with more fully in Chapter 3.

In the example above the proprietor did not finance the whole business himself, but borrowed £50,000 from another source. Apart from this, the rest of the business belongs to him, so his own capital is now £68,000.

If, during the course of the next few weeks, the whole of the stocks were sold for £2,000, the dual effect would be:

Stocks reduced by £2,000
Debtors (or cash) increased by £2,000

There would be no change in the amount of net assets, which would still be £118,000, and the proprietor's capital would still be £68,000. All that has happened is that one asset has been exchanged for another at the same value.

If, on the other hand, the whole of the stocks were sold for £5,000 (i.e. at a profit of £3,000), there would be the additional matter of the profit to record. The net assets would have increased by £3,000, and so would the proprietor's capital. Assuming that the sales were for cash, a new balance sheet prepared after the changes would look like this:

Assets	£	£
Premises		80,000
Furniture and equipment		30,000
China and glass		4,000
Stocks of food and wine		–
Debtors		1,000
Cash at bank and in hand		12,000
		127,000
Less liabilities due for imminent payment		6,000
		121,000
Financed by:		
Proprietor's capital as at 31 October	68,000	
Add profit since then	3,000	
		71,000
Borrowed capital		50,000
		121,000

In practice we could not prepare a new balance sheet after each transaction, nor calculate the profit on each transaction. The very many individual transactions would be recorded day by day in the books, and the net effect summarised in a profit and loss account and a balance sheet at the end of the year. The profit shown by the profit and loss account *for the year* will be reflected in the amount of the proprietor's capital shown by the balance sheet *as at the end of the year*.

Exercises

1 State whether the following transactions represent assets, expenses, liabilities, or income of a hotel:

(a) Cost of kitchen equipment.
(b) Cost of cleaning materials used.
(c) Amounts owing to suppliers.
(d) Sales of meals.
(e) Rent payable.
(f) Charges to guests for accommodation.
(g) Cost of maintenance.
(h) Bank overdraft.

2 Set out the following balances from the books of account of a restaurant in the form of a trial balance as at 31 March 19..

	£
Sales of meals	112,900
Cost of food	44,800
Wages of staff	31,100
Rent paid	6,800
Other expenses	21,600
Furniture and equipment	42,000
Debtors	1,300
Creditors	4,700
Cash at bank	8,200
Stocks of food	700
Proprietor's capital at beginning of year	38,900

3 The following list of balances comes from the books of a hotel. Set them out in the form of a trial balance as at 31 October 19.., and then prepare a profit and loss account for the year ended 31 October 19.. and a balance sheet as at that date.

	£
Cost of hotel building	180,000
Takings	102,600
Furniture	18,400
Debtors	1,500
Kitchen equipment	25,000
China and glass	4,200
Creditors	9,300
Wages	30,100
Cash at bank	8,900
Cost of food	19,800
Loan from bank	80,000
Expenses	39,600
Proprietor's capital at beginning of the year	135,600

2 Double-entry book-keeping

At the heart of all double-entry book-keeping is the ledger, consisting of many accounts of different kinds of financial transactions. An account is a record of all the transactions of one particular kind, such as sales, cash owned, rent payable, or the amount owing to a supplier. With the development of computers, and particularly personal computers being within the scope of even small businesses, it is now common for this information to be recorded electronically. Originally, however, the ledger was handwritten in a large book, each page being divided vertically into two sides, referred to as the debit side and the credit side. The double entry consists of one entry on the debit (left-hand) side of one account, and one entry on the credit (right-hand) side of another account. An understanding of this basic principle will be a great help in dealing with financial information whether it is recorded on paper or micro-chips.

Cash transactions

If cash is received, one of the accounts will be cash account, and an entry will be made on the debit side (receive with your left hand); the corresponding entry on the credit side of another account will be a record of what the money was received for. If cash is paid out, an entry will be made on the credit side of cash account (pay out with your right hand), and the corresponding entry made on the debit side of another account to show what the payment was made for.

Example

June 1   A. Pieman starts in business with £500 in cash.
     1   He buys pies for resale for £85 cash.
     2   Equipment purchased for £30 cash.
     3   Paid travelling expenses to fair £6.
     4   Sold all his pies for £125 cash.

Cash account

	£			£
June 1 Capital account	500		June 1 Purchases	85
4 Sales	125		2 Equipment	30
			3 Travelling expenses	6
			4 Balance carried down	504
	625			625
June 5 Balance brought down	504			

A. Pieman Capital account

		June 1 Cash account	500

Purchases account

June 1 Cash account	85

Equipment account

June 2 Cash account	30

Travelling expenses account

June 3 Cash account	6

Sales account

		June 4 Cash account	125

Trial balance at 4 June 19..

	Dr £	Cr £
Cash	504	
Capital – A. Pieman		500
Purchases	85	
Equipment	30	
Travelling expenses	6	
Sales		125
	625	625

Notes

1 The cash account is balanced off (both sides totalled and the balance entered as a double entry between the old period and the start of the new period), but it is not necessary with the other accounts because, in this example, there is only one entry on each account, which is therefore the balance on that account. In computer records the balance (the difference between total debits and total credits on the account) will be shown automatically.

2 The first double entry is between cash account and capital account, recording the receiving of £500 by the business (left hand), and giving of £500 (right hand) by the proprietor to the business. Since the business has £500 of the

proprietor's, he is a creditor of the business, which is shown by an entry on the credit side of his account.

3   Notice that purchases of pies are distinguished from purchases of equipment. The pies are goods for resale, and the cost will be taken into account when calculating profit, but the equipment is a fixed asset, which will assist in earning the profit but does not form part of the trade, i.e. the business is not that of buying and selling equipment. The word 'purchases' will be used in all book-keeping and accounts to mean only purchases of goods for resale, so that confusion does not arise.

4   Since there has been a double entry made for every item recorded, the total debit entries must equal the total credit entries. Similarly the effect of balancing the cash account is to deduct £121 from both sides, so the total of balances on the debit side must equal the total of balances on the credit side. This is proved by setting out the trial balance, which at the same time checks the balancing and lists the financial information needed for preparing a profit and loss account and a balance sheet.

Cash book

It will be seen that the entries in the cash account were more numerous than in any other account, and accordingly in handwritten account books it was customary to keep the cash account separate in another book called the cash book, so that the ledger now consisted of two volumes, the cash book and the general ledger. In practice it is usual for so-called cash transactions to be conducted by cheques drawn on a bank, and payments of actual cash to be restricted to small items referred to as petty cash.

Computer records

The computer deals with debits and credits by recording them as plus or minus entries on each account. So the cash account in the above example would print out like this:

Cash account

			£
June 1	Capital		500
1	Purchases		−85
2	Equipment		−30
3	Travelling expenses		−6
4	Sales		125
4	Balance		504

It is often helpful in working out whether a particular entry is a debit or a credit if it is reasoned from the entry in cash account, where it is easy to remember that cash is received with the left hand and paid out with the right hand. Whichever side a transaction should be entered on cash account, the principle of double entry means that the entry on the other account will be on the other side. Thus an entry on printing and stationery account will be on the opposite side from the payment appearing in cash account (credit side), so it must be on the debit side. Since printing and stationery is an expense, we would expect the entries to be on the debit side of the account, as explained in Chapter 1.

When making handwritten entries in a ledger, it was important to make them on the correct side of the correct account if the information recorded was to be accurate. When making entries into a computer, it is still essential to identify the account correctly, but deciding whether the entry is a plus or minus to the total on that account is comparatively simple.

Credit transactions

Credit transactions are those resulting in a debt which will be settled later. In a restaurant most sales will be cash transactions, with only some customers charging their meals to an account. Purchases on the other hand are likely to be mostly made on credit, suppliers being paid monthly for all purchases made during the previous month. Hotels extend limited credit to their guests for the period of their stay, settlement usually being made when the guest departs. Purchases by the hotel will be on monthly credit as with a restaurant.

It is advisable to record every credit transaction when it happens, even though no cash has changed hands at that time. The purchase or sale is the same whether paid for or not; only the other half of the double entry is different, with the creation of a debt being substituted for the cash. The cash is paid later, not for the original reason (purchase of goods) but to settle a debt. For a business constantly repeating orders to suppliers it is of course much more convenient not to pay for each item separately, but to collect them up and pay for several at once. As far as the book-keeping is concerned, it means recording each new debt, of which the creditor must advise the debtor by means of an invoice, and then later recording settlement of the accumulated total, probably allowing for cash discount.

Example

During the month of May, purchases by the Exotic Hotel were as follows:

May 1 Purchases on credit from Brown Ltd £453.
     5 Purchases on credit from Jones Ltd £537.
    11 Cash purchases £17.
    19 Purchases on credit from Brown Ltd £372.
    22 Goods returned to Jones Ltd £48.
    24 Purchases on credit from Canned Foods Ltd £726.
    31 Purchases on credit from Jones Ltd £691.

Note that in a real business there would be no convenient list of transactions available from which to write up the records. The information would come from invoices received from the suppliers in respect of credit purchases, and cheque-book counterfoils or cash receipts for cash purchases.

During the month £17 is credited to cash account (money paid out) and the other items amounting to £2,731 credited to the accounts of the various creditors.

	£
Credited to Brown Ltd	453
Jones Ltd	537
Brown Ltd	372
Debited to Jones Ltd	−48
Credited to Canned Foods Ltd	726
Jones Ltd	691
	2731

A handwritten set of books would list these items in a purchases day book before entering them in the ledger, so that only the total for the month need be entered on purchases account. All the individual amounts would be entered on the suppliers' accounts.

At the end of the month the amounts recorded will be as follows:

Cash account balance will be reduced by £17.

		£	£
Purchases account	(Debit)	2,748	
Brown Ltd account	(Credit)		825
Jones Ltd account	(Credit)		1,180
Canned Foods Ltd account	(Credit)		726

The three credit balances on the *personal accounts* represent the creditors of the business (i.e. the debts owing by the business) at 31 May.

Discounts

It is usual for creditors to encourage prompt payment by offering a so-called cash discount for payment within a specified time. A discount of 2½ per cent if payment is made by the 17th of the month following the invoice date is common. The result is that a debt shown as £100 will be settled by a payment of £97.50 if paid promptly, and the book-keeping records will need to show this.

In order to have the information available when entering the transactions it is essential to note on the cheque-book counterfoil not only the amount of the cheque, but also the amount of discount deducted. When the payment is entered in the books, the cheque and discount will both be debited to the creditor's account, thus cancelling the record of the debt.

The amounts of discount will be listed for credit to discounts received account. In handwritten books this listing will be done in the cash book alongside the amounts paid, and the total of discounts for the month entered in discounts account in one sum. It is a credit to the account because the account is a record of income which has been earned by paying promptly. Also it needs to be a credit in order to complete the double entry if the individual amounts of discount were entered on the debit side of the suppliers' accounts.

Canned Foods Ltd

		£	£
June 1	Balance brought forward		−726 Cr
17	Cash	708	
	Discount	18	
			726
			NIL

Example

At 1 April the assets and liabilities of O. Henry trading as the Acorn Restaurant were: Premises £68,000; Furniture and equipment £17,230; Stock of food £482; Account owing by Borstal Golf Club for credit sales £174; Owing to Allfoods Ltd £960; Bank overdraft £2,381; and Loan from Business Finance PLC £55,000. During April the following transactions took place:

April 2 Purchases on credit from Allfoods Ltd £1,287.
  4 Paid sundry expenses by cheque £29.
  11 Received cheque from Borstal Golf Club £174.
  14 Paid Allfoods March account less 2½ per cent cash discount.
  17 Banked takings £3,948.
  20 Purchases paid by cheque £110.
  23 Purchases on credit from Allfoods Ltd £1,325.
  28 Drew cheque for wages and salaries £1,956.
  29 Banked takings £4,073.
  30 Cheque cashed by proprietor O. Henry for private use £200.

Working

Note that the balance on O. Henry's capital account at 1 April will be the net total of assets belonging to him, i.e.

	£	£
		68,000
		17,230
		482
		174
		85,886
Less Liabilities	960	
	2,381	
	55,000	58,341
		27,545

O. Henry Capital a/c

	April 1 Balance	27,545

Business Finance PLC loan a/c

	April 1 Balance	55,000

Bank a/c

		£			£
April 11	Borstal G.C.	174	April 1	Balance	
17	Takings	3,948		O/drawn	2,381
29	Takings	4,073	4	Sundry expenses	29
			14	Allfoods Ltd	936
			20	Purchases	110
			28	Wages and salaries	1,956
			30	Drawings	200
			30	Balance in hand	2,583
		8,195			8,195

May 1 Balance in hand 2,583

Premises a/c

April 1 Balance	68,000	

Furniture and equipment a/c

April 1 Balance	17,230	

Stock a/c

April 1 Balance	482	

Borstal Golf Club a/c

April 1 Balance	174	April 11 Bank	174

Allfoods Ltd

April 14	Bank	936	April 1	Balance	960
14	Discount	24	April 2	Purchases	1,287
30	Balance	2,612	April 23	Purchases	1,325
		3,572			3,572
			May 1	Balance	2,612

Purchases a/c

April 2	Allfoods Ltd	1,287
20	Bank	110
23	Allfoods Ltd	1,325

Sundry expenses a/c

April 4	Bank	29

Discounts received a/c

	£			£
		April 30	Allfoods Ltd	24

Takings a/c

		£
April 17	Bank	3,948
29	Bank	4,073

Wages and salaries a/c

April 28 Bank   1,956

Drawings a/c

April 30 Bank   200

Trial balance at 30 April 19..

	Dr £	Cr £
O. Henry capital		27,545
Business Finance PLC loan		55,000
Bank	2,583	
Premises	68,000	
Furniture and equipment	17,230	
Stock in hand	482	
Allfoods Ltd		2,612
Purchases	2,722	
Sundry expenses	29	
Discounts received		24
Takings		8,021
Wages and salaries	1,956	
Drawings	200	
	93,202	93,202

In this example there were very few transactions, so each double entry was shown separately. In practice some transactions would be very numerous, and would more conveniently be listed before entering in the ledger. Credit purchases, for example, would be listed in a purchases day book, and only the total of all such items for the month would be entered in purchases account, although each item would be entered in the suppliers' personal accounts. Similarly payments to all suppliers would be subject to discount, which would be listed in the cash book and only the total for the month credited to discounts received account.

Purchases account and takings account have not been balanced off, although they each have more than one entry, because they will be added to throughout the year until a profit and loss account is prepared. Until then only a pencil running total will be used for finding the amount to enter in the trial balance.

Hotel charges and deposits

The traditional hotel tabular ledger was designed to be a combination of sales day book (a list of credit sales) and customers' ledger (showing the indebtedness of each customer). The guests' balances are debits (the debtors of the hotel), and the amounts charged in making up those balances are shown in analysis columns to facilitate adding up and posting in total to the credit of the various income accounts (accommodation charges, restaurant takings, bar takings) in the general ledger. Again debits and credits are of equal amount. Entering the dockets for everything charged to guests must be kept up to date whether they are entered in a tabular ledger or a computer. Either way the amount due from a guest must be immediately ascertainable so that his bill can be rendered when required.

One aspect which is special to hotels is the advance booking deposit. When an intending guest pays a deposit for a future booking, the double entry is debit cash account (cash received), and credit advance booking deposits account (debts owed to future guests). When the time of the booking arrives, the deposit becomes part of the payment of the guest's account, and a transfer must be made in the books to debit advance booking deposits account and credit the guest account.

Exercises

1   What account should be debited and what account credited to complete the double-entry for each of the following trans-actions?
(a) Purchases bought for cash £15.
(b) Additional furniture bought for cash £350.
(c) Replacement cutlery £115 bought on credit from Silver-ware Ltd.
(d) Cash sales of meals £78.
(e) Deposit £50 received on 17 May for hotel booking in July.
(f) Foodstuffs costing £53 bought on credit from Jenks Ltd.
2   Show the entries in a handwritten ledger to record the following information at 30th September 19.. (Note that the proprietor's capital account balance should also be entered.)

Balance at bank £2,745.
Amounts owing to suppliers: £1,270 to Jones Ltd; £890 to Brown & Co.
Amount due from Anglers' Association for annual dinner £478.
Freehold premises owned £85,000.
Furniture and fittings £7,840.
Kitchen equipment £8,920.
Stock of food £589.
Loan from Merchant Bank PLC £75,000.

3 J. Bloggs opened a restaurant on 1 October with a capital of £10,000, represented by Furniture and equipment £5,620, Cutlery, china and glass £700, Bank balance £3,940, and a debt of £260 to Cooks Ltd for food purchased. His transactions during October were as follows:

Oct. 1 Purchases of food paid by cheque £74.
       2 Paid rent by cheque £370.
       3 Purchased food on credit from Cooks Ltd £315.
       7 Banked takings £975.
       8 Cheque drawn for wages £410.
      10 Paid cheque for printing and stationery £38.
      12 Purchased food on credit from Farmers Ltd £528.
      14 Banked takings £1,320.
      15 Cheque drawn for wages £410.
      15 Purchased food on credit from Cooks Ltd £495.
      18 Cheque paid for sundry expenses £17.
      21 Banked takings £1,240.
      22 Cheque drawn for wages £410.
      23 Purchased food on credit from Farmers Ltd £611.
      28 Banked takings £1,534.
      29 Cheque drawn for wages £410.
      31 Purchased food on credit from Cooks Ltd £593.

Show the ledger entries to record the opening entries of capital, assets, and liability, and the transactions during October.

3   *The balance sheet*

The assets, liabilities, and capital of a business at a given date represent the financial state of the business at that date. If the amounts are grouped together under suitable headings in the form of a balance sheet, they will constitute a financial statement showing the worth of the business, and provide information from which conclusions may be deduced about its financial strength.

Assets do not all have the same relevance to the business. Some are part of the actual trade, being converted into and out of cash as part of the daily activity. These are referred to as *current assets*, and comprise stocks, debtors, and money balances. Other assets are acquired in order to assist in running the business, but do not form part of the trade itself. They are called *fixed assets*, and include premises, kitchen equipment, furniture and fittings, office equipment, vehicles, and are usually owned for a number of years. Thus a restaurant owns kitchen equipment in order to assist in the business of selling meals, not as part of the trade of buying and selling kitchen equipment.

In a balance sheet, it is customary to show assets grouped into fixed assets and current assets, and also to put individual types of assets into the *order of realisability*, or the order in which they are likely to be converted into cash. Premises are likely to be held longest, followed possibly by equipment and then vehicles. Of the current assets, stock is sold to become debtors, debtors pay and become cash, so the order of realisability is stock, debtors, and then cash.

Those liabilities which must be paid very soon are called *current liabilities*, and are shown in the balance sheet as a deduction from the current assets out of which they must be paid. The remaining balance of current assets after deducting current liabilities is the *working capital* of the business, or that part of the total capital which is available for day-to-day working, and not locked up in fixed assets.

Equity capital is that part of the capital used in the business which belongs to the proprietors. The capital put into the business, and the profits left in the business, give the proprietors an *equity* or right of ownership, and the total of the two amounts is known as equity capital.

Consider the following example:

FOUNTAIN RESTAURANT LTD
Balance Sheet as at 31 March 19..

	£	£
Employment of Capital		
Fixed Assets		
Leasehold premises		19,000
Furniture and equipment		4,000
Crockery, cutlery and glass		700
		23,700

	£	£
Current Assets		
Stock	900	
Debtors	300	
Cash	4,300	
	5,500	
Less Current Liabilities		
Creditors	3,900	
Working capital		1,600
Net assets of the company		25,300
Sources of Capital		
Share Capital		20,000
Reserves		
Unappropriated profit		5,300
Total Shareholders' Capital (or Equity Capital)		25,300

The illustration is of a limited company, which means that the business has been registered as a company with the Registrar of Companies, and in fact the Companies Acts would require the balance sheet to be set out in more detail than in this simple form. The effect on the balance sheet of being a company concerns only the way in which the proprietors' capital is shown, allowing for the fact that there may be a great many proprietors. Their individual proportions of capital are recorded in the books as so many shares of the total share capital, but the individual shareholdings are not shown in the balance sheet.

If there had been only one proprietor, or *sole trader*, instead of a company, his capital would have been shown as one amount due to him, including the profits made and after deducting *drawings*, or amounts withdrawn from the business by him. He is in business to earn his livelihood, and he will usually draw regular amounts to live on, which reduce the amount by which the profits would otherwise increase his capital. The part of the balance sheet dealing with net assets would be the same as for a company, because the business would have the same assets as if it were a company. Only the source of capital would be different. See the following:

FOUNTAIN RESTAURANT
(P. Bloggs Proprietor)
Balance Sheet as at 31 March 19..

	£	£
Employment of Capital		
Fixed Assets		
Leasehold premises		19,000
Furniture and equipment		4,000
Crockery, cutlery and glass		700
		23,700

	£	£
Current Assets		
Stock	900	
Debtors	300	
Cash	4,300	
	5,500	
Less Current Liabilities		
Creditors	3,900	
Working capital		1,600
Net assets		25,300
Sources of Capital		
P. Bloggs capital account as last year		22,900
Add net profit for the year		6,600
		29,500
Less drawings during the year		4,200
		25,300

The profit £6,600 shown in P. Bloggs capital account is the net profit made by the business in the year ended on the balance sheet date, and as it belongs to P. Bloggs, it has the effect of increasing his capital in the business. Because of the profit-making, the net assets will also be £6,600 more than they were last year. On the other hand, the proprietor's drawings have reduced the net assets by £4,200, and his capital is correspondingly less.

In the case of the company the capital £20,000 represented by the issue of shares may remain unchanged year by year. It is the amount of capital put into the company by the shareholders, as distinct from extra capital arising from profits left in by them, and will be shown unchanged in the balance sheet. The extra capital caused by accumulated profit less dividends to the shareholders is shown as a separate amount under the heading *reserves*, which is the term used for any extra shareholders' capital over and above the share capital.

If the business had been owned by two or more persons in partnership, the owners' capital would have been shown divided between the partners. Again the net assets *of the business* would not be affected; only the source of capital [i.e. the ownership] would be different, and this difference would be reflected in the balance sheet, as follows:

FOUNTAIN RESTAURANT
(P. Bloggs and F. Blodgett)
Balance Sheet as at 31 March 19..

	£	£	£
Employment of Capital			
Fixed Assets			
Leasehold premises			19,000
Furniture and equipment			4,000
Crockery, cutlery and glass			700
			23,700

	£	£	£
Current Assets			
Stock		900	
Debtors		300	
Cash		4,300	
		5,500	
Less Current Liabilities			
Creditors		3,900	
Working capital			1,600
Net assets			25,300

Sources of Capital			
Partners' capital accounts	*Bloggs*	*Blodgett*	
Balance as last year	14,200	8,700	22,900
Add share of net profits	4,400	2,200	6,600
	18,600	10,900	29,500
Less drawings	2,200	2,000	4,200
	16,400	8,900	25,300

The capital of partners is sometimes shown with the original amounts contributed by the partners separate from the extra capital arising from profits less drawings, in the same way as the company share capital was separated from the reserves. The fluctuating parts of the capital of the partners arising from their shares of profits less drawings are referred to as their *current accounts*, as follows:

	Bloggs	*Blodgett*	
Sources of Capital	£	£	£
Partners' capital accounts	13,000	7,000	20,000
Partners' Current Accounts:			
Balance as last year	1,200	1,700	
Add share of profit	4,400	2,200	
	5,600	3,900	
Less drawings	2,200	2,000	
	3,400	1,900	5,300
			25,300

Fixed rate capital

Proprietors do not always provide all the capital needed by the business out of their own pockets. Some capital may be borrowed, privately or from a bank or finance house. Such borrowed capital will not entitle the lender to a share in profits, but to a fixed rate of interest to be paid every year while the loan remains unrepaid, whether the business has made a profit or not. To the business the interest is an expense, and money borrowed is *loan capital* or *fixed rate capital*, to distinguish it from owners' or equity capital.

A bank overdraft is not usually regarded as loan capital but as a current liability, because of the short-term nature of the arrangement with the bank. An overdraft is not a loan, but an arrangement with the bank permitting the current account to be overdrawn within stated limits for a stated time. It may continue for many years by constant renewal of the arrangement with the bank, but the point is that the arrangement does need renewing; at no time is it guaranteed for a long enough period to constitute capital. If each arrangement is for a period of 3 months, there is always the possibility of the overdraft being called in at the end of that time, and it is consequently a current liability for the purposes of the balance sheet. This is in contrast to a bank *loan* given for a stated period of years, which can therefore be properly regarded as capital for that time.

When there is more capital available to the business than is required for the purposes of the trade, it may be that investment will be made outside the business. Investments may be *general* investments, made as a way of utilising surplus cash to earn an income, or *trade* investments made to promote the trade itself. The latter may take the form of investing in another business whose trade can profitably be linked with our own. So far as the balance sheet is concerned, investments fall somewhere between fixed assets and current assets, and should be shown in that way between the two.

Taxation owing at the balance sheet date may include amounts for VAT, income tax, and corporation tax. VAT will be payable whether the business is owned by a sole proprietor, a partnership, or a company, and will be a current liability. Tax on the profits of a business owned by a sole proprietor or a partnership will not normally show in the accounts, as it is the personal responsibility of the individual owner(s). Any payment of tax through the business is treated as private drawings.

Corporation tax is paid on the profits of any organisation other than individuals, partnerships, or trusts, and this of course includes companies. Some tax may be payable soon after the balance sheet date, and this will be a current liability. Some tax may not be payable for some long time, and this is referred to as a deferred liability and shown separately. We will look further into this in Chapter 9 on companies.

Goodwill

There have been many different attempts to define goodwill, and they all boil down to meaning the value of a going concern over and above the value of the other assets. If a business has premises, equipment and stock worth £180,000, and a purchaser is willing to pay £200,000 for it, then the goodwill is worth £20,000. The extra value will have much to do with the fact that the business is already a going concern making profits, which is more attractive than just a collection of assets with no past history and connections.

When a business has been built up from nothing, there will have been no payment to a previous proprietor for goodwill, so no amount will appear in the balance sheet. If the business has been purchased for a sum including goodwill, then the balance sheet of the new proprietor will include goodwill as a fixed asset (perhaps the most fixed of all!), but even then it is quite common to write off the amount against subsequent profits in order to get rid of it from the balance sheet. The reason usually given for this is that the value of goodwill is constantly changing with the profitability of the business, and it might embarrass possible future negotiations to have an out-of-date figure perpetuated in the balance sheet.

The whole subject of goodwill can become complicated, particularly when the value has to be estimated without an actual sale (as on a change of partnership). It is usual to base such estimates on profitability, but these complications are not part of hotel and catering management and need not concern us here.

Balance sheet date

We have talked about the balance sheet date, and the accounting year or financial year ending on that date, and it may be wondered how that date is decided. There is no law or regulation governing this, and it is not necessary to make accounts up to the end of the income tax year on 5 April. It is likely that accounts will just be prepared for the year from when the business was started, and thereafter annually on the same date. However, if a different date is more relevant to the nature of the business, e.g. 30 September for a seasonal seaside hotel, the proprietors may very well make this their annual balance sheet date. Whatever date is decided upon, it will not normally be changed again without a very good reason.

Exercises

1 Explain the difference between equity capital and fixed rate capital.
2 What is meant by the term 'reserves' in the balance sheet of a company?
3 Prepare a balance sheet from the following balances in the books of the Cliff Hotel as at 31 March 19.. :

	£	£
Proprietor's capital at beginning of year		47,200
Cash drawn by proprietor during year	14,700	
Hotel premises	97,300	
Bank loan		80,000
Furniture and equipment	23,800	
Motor van	3,700	
Stocks of food and wine	600	

	£	£
Sundry debtors and amounts due from guests	1,800	
Sundry creditors		5,900
Balance at bank	6,400	
Cash float	200	
Net profit for the year		15,400
	148,500	148,500

4   From the following balances, prepare a balance sheet as at
31 October 19.. for the Dene Hotel owned by J. Bloggs and
D. Bloggs in partnership:

	£	£
Capital account – J. Bloggs		50,000
Capital account – D. Bloggs		30,000
Hotel premises	149,300	
Furniture and equipment	31,700	
Motor van	4,200	
Sundry debtors and creditors	3,100	7,900
Stocks of food and wines	900	
Balance at bank	8,600	
Mortgage loan from Terra Finance PLC		100,000
Current account at beginning of year – J. Bloggs		7,100
Current account at beginning of year – D. Bloggs		3,200
Share of profits – J. Bloggs		16,800
– D. Bloggs		12,600
Drawings during the past year – J. Bloggs	15,800	
– D. Bloggs	14,000	
	227,600	227,600

4 Income and expenditure

Income is the value of amounts earned by using resources. It is referred to as revenue, and will be taken into account in calculating whether a profit has been made. It has the effect of increasing capital, since it gives the right to assets which were not previously owned. It is derived from selling goods or services, and will include such items as sales of stock, accommodation charges, miscellaneous charges to customers, rents receivable, investment income, and discounts received. Sums received in exchange for assets which were previously held as part of the business capital, such as the sale of an old refrigerator, are capital receipts, not revenue, and except for adjustments of depreciation will not be taken into account in calculating profit. The amounts of all items of income will appear on the credit, or right-hand side of the trial balance.

Expenses, or revenue expenditure, are outgoings incurred in order to earn the revenue, and do not add to the assets. They will be set off against the revenue in calculating whether a profit has been made, and will include cost of goods sold, wages and salaries, rent, rates, insurance (i.e. the premiums payable), bank charges, cleaning and laundry, repairs and maintenance of premises and equipment, and all other outgoings incurred in running the business. Revenue expenditure must be distinguished from capital expenditure, which is incurred in adding to the value of fixed assets or obtaining new capital. A business is likely to have more items of expense than of income, and the amounts of all expenditure will appear on the debit, or left-hand side, of the trial balance.

A profit and loss account collects together all the totals of different kinds of income and expenses shown in the trial balance, and sets them off against one another to show whether the result is a profit or a loss for the period covered by the account. Consider the following:

Trial Balance at 30 September 19..

	Dr £	Cr £
Various assets	119,900	
Various liabilities		11,200
Capital, as last year		98,400
Sales		103,500
Cost of food sold	41,400	
Wages and salaries	26,700	
Heating and lighting	7,600	

	£	£
Rates	3,800	
Insurance	2,300	
Printing, stationery and telephone	2,900	
Advertising and display	1,800	
Miscellaneous expenses	2,400	
Depreciation of fixed assets	4,300	
	213,100	213,100

In this simple example, the capital, assets, and liabilities, which will all be shown in the balance sheet, have been abridged into the first three items, and the headings of income and expenses are the remaining items.

Profit and Loss account for the year ended 30th September 19..

	£	£
Sales		103,500
Less expenses:		
Cost of food sold	41,400	
Wages and salaries	26,700	
Heating and lighting	7,600	
Rates	3,800	
Insurance	2,300	
Printing, stationery and telephone	2,900	
Advertising and display	1,800	
Miscellaneous expenses	2,400	
Depreciation of fixed assets	4,300	
		93,200
Net profit for the year		10,300

The net profit belongs to the proprietor, and will be added to his capital account, but it also follows that the net assets must be that much greater than they were last year when the capital was £98,400. So the net assets (assets less liabilities) now must be £10,300 more than £98,400, or a new total of £108,700. Try it by going back to the trial balance and deducting the liabilities from the assets!

Gross profit is the term used for the profit before deducting the expenses of running the business, allowing only for the cost of goods sold. In the above example the gross profit would be £62,100 (sales £103,500, less cost of food sold £41,400), and it is usual to prepare the profit and loss account to show the gross profit, before going on to show the expenses and the net profit. This first part of the account is called the *trading account*, because it is an account of the trading (buying and selling of goods) without including details of the expenses of doing so. It is important because the cost of goods sold should remain in proportion to the amounts charged for them (sales), and vice versa, and this can be confirmed by expressing the one as a percentage of the other.

*Trading and Profit and Loss account
for the year ended 30 September 19..*

	£	£
Sales		103,500
Less cost of food sold		41,400
Gross profit (60)%		62,100
Less expenses:		
Wages and salaries	26,700	
Heating and lighting	7,600	
Rates	3,800	
Insurance	2,300	
Printing, stationery and telephone	2,900	
Advertising and display	1,800	
Miscellaneous expenses	2,400	
Depreciation of fixed assets	4,300	
		51,800
Net profit for the year		10,300

The cost of the food that has been sold during the year will not be found in the ledger, ready for inclusion in the trading account. What we find in the ledger will be an account of the food purchased during the year, which can never be arranged to be exactly the amount we need for the meals sold. There will always need to be an adjustment for the stock of food left in the stores ready for use, at the beginning of the period as well as at the end, and also for the cost of meals supplied to staff. The purchases will include the cost of food which has not been sold but has been used for staff meals. This is a cost to the business, but it is not part of the cost of food sold. It is part of labour cost, and should be deducted from food cost and added to labour cost. See the following:

	£	£
Sales		103,500
Less cost of food sold		
Stock in hand at beginning of the year	2,800	
Add purchases during the year	40,900	
	43,700	
Less stock in hand at end of the year	2,300	
	41,400	
Less staff meals	3,200	38,200
Gross profit		65,300

Discounts

A discount may be merely a reduction in the price of goods, perhaps given by a wholesaler to a retailer as part of the normal terms of trade. This kind of discount is called a *trade discount*, and the accounting treatment is to record only the net amount charged, ignoring the original amount quoted and the discount. The purpose of such a discount is to enable price lists to be prepared with retail prices for display to the ultimate customers. To the middleman the purchase price is the net amount after discount, and this is the only figure he will record.

Another kind of discount which *will* be recorded is *cash discount*, which is given if payment of a debt is made within a stated time. This discount is not a reduction of the purchase price, but a reduction of the payment if it is made promptly. It is not allowed automatically, it has to be earned by being prompt, so it is another form of income which a business can earn. Some types of business will earn discounts received from their creditors, and also incur the expense of discounts allowed to their debtors, but it is likely that only discounts received will be found in the accounts of a catering business. It should be shown in the profit and loss account after gross profit and before deducting the expenses. If there are any discounts allowed, they should be shown in the profit and loss account along with all the other expenses. They are not set off against discounts received, as they are nothing to do with one another. One is income earned by deliberately paying promptly, the other is an expense incurred to encourage our own debtors to settle quickly.

For the moment we are concerning ourselves only with the form of the account and its preparation, but we must not forget that the purpose behind it all is to convey information about the business. We shall see later what sort of information we shall look for, but one aspect already mentioned is the percentage of gross profit to sales. It is very important to check this regularly, and the figures will only be dependable if the items recorded as sales and purchases include only sales of meals and purchases of food for the meals sold. Similarly, when we come to look at bar profits, sales and purchases must mean only sales of bar stocks and purchases of bar stocks. For accounting purposes, sales and purchases of anything but stocks must always be described in full as 'sales of equipment', or 'purchases of cleaning materials', or whatever the item is.

In preparing the profit and loss account the order of expense items is not vital, but it is usual to start with the cost of employing staff, which is the biggest single item, and then show the cost of occupying the premises. Similarly there will always be some 'odds and ends' description, such as 'sundry expenses' or 'miscellaneous expenses' to cover all those small items which are not big or important enough to show separately, and this or depreciation will usually be shown last. The question of depreciation will be dealt with in Chapter 6.

Exercises

1 (a) State what adjustment should be made to the figures in preparing a trading and profit and loss account, in respect of the cost of staff meals included in purchases.
   (b) Why is it necessary to make this adjustment?

(c) Would the gross profit percentage appear to be better or worse if no adjustment were made?

2 Sales of meals in a restaurant amounted to £147,300 last year, and purchases of food amounted to £59,320. Food stocks at the beginning of the year amounted to £1,140 and at the end of the year were £1,280. The cost of food used for staff meals was £1,733. Set out a trading account for the year to find the gross profit made, and calculate the gross profit percentage of sales.

3 Briefly explain what is meant by:

    (a) Discount received
    (b) Capital receipts
    (c) Revenue expenditure
    (d) Gross profit
    (e) Capital expenditure

4 The following figures were extracted from the books of a restaurant for the year ended 31 March 19..

	£
Sales	102,600
Purchases	41,060
Stock of food at beginning of year	320
Stock of food at end of year	960
Wages	18,760
Salaries	16,660
Rates and insurance	5,840
Lighting and heating	2,620
Maintenance and repairs	1,880
Renewals	1,160
Depreciation	1,520
Sundry expenses	1,070

Prepare a trading and profit and loss account for the year, making adjustment for the cost of staff meals of £1,440 included in purchases.

5 Accounting concepts and conventions

Understanding an account of the use of funds must depend on some acceptance of guidelines by which the information is presented, and these guidelines are *accounting concepts*. Any departure from these concepts (such as revaluation of fixed assets) should be carefully noted in the accounts to avoid misunderstanding.

Cost concept

The amounts recorded on acquiring assets of the business will be the original cost to the business, and assets will continue to be recorded at this value unless otherwise stated.

Business entity concept

The business is treated as a separate entity from its owner. Although the owner or proprietor may perform all the actions undertaken for the business, they are recorded only so far as they affect the business, and the proprietor is treated as a creditor of the business so far as his capital in the business is concerned.

Dual aspect concept

Every transaction has a dual aspect of funds, goods, or services leaving one place and being received at another, and both aspects need to be recorded if accounting is to be complete. Double entry is the method of recording the transaction so that the dual aspect is taken into account.

Going concern concept

The treatment of all items recorded will be on the basis of the business continuing. So an item of specialist equipment which may be worthless if it had to be sold off may still be recorded as valuable to the business.

Accruals concept

This allows for the difference between income and expenditure relating to a period and the cash received and paid out in that period. The cash received may include amounts relating to a previous period but received late, and amounts such as deposits received in respect of some future period. It may not include amounts relating to this period but not yet received. Similarly the payments may differ from the amounts due to be paid for this period.

Money measurement concept

All transactions shall be capable of being measured in terms of money. There may be other aspects of the business which are of interest, but the information contained in accounts is concerned only with what can be expressed in money terms.

Realisation concept

This is particularly related to profits, which should not be taken into account until they are realised, or turned into cash. So if the business holds stock which is now worth more than when it was purchased, no account of the increased value is taken until it is sold. This avoids the danger of over-optimism, which might lead to assuming a profit that is never realised.

Materiality concept

Accounting records will use headings for groups of transactions, and for any particular business the headings will be such as are important to that business. If the nature or amount of an item is not material, i.e. important to the business, it will be grouped with other items instead of being shown separately.

Prudence concept

When there are possible alternative views about the treatment of an item in accounts, the most prudent view shall be adopted. If there is a choice of values to be placed on entries recorded, the prudence concept ensures that the value used will show the least profitability. It is the basis of the practice of taking into account all probable losses, but ignoring probable profits until they become fact.

Consistency concept

In considering the application of accounting concepts it often happens that more than one reasonable interpretation can be applied. For instance, the question of depreciation of fixed assets can be dealt with in different ways. When there are alternative views about the accounting for an item, a decision should be made about which treatment should be adopted, and then consistently adhered to.

6 Depreciation of fixed assets

If an article is purchased during the financial year and used up or disposed of before the end of the year, the cost of the article is an expense of the year and will be included in the calculation of profit or loss. A fixed asset, however, will usually be owned and in use for several years, and it would be wrong to treat the cost as an expense of only 1 year. In the annual accounts the amount of capital employed in providing the fixed assets, so far as it has not been used up, will be shown in the balance sheet. However, it would be equally wrong to show the whole of the original cost in this way if use of the asset during the year has used up some of the cost.

A fixed asset, such as a motor van bought for £5,000, may be used for 4 years and then disposed of for £1,000. The loss of capital incurred in the 4 years is therefore £4,000, and part of this loss should be shown in the accounts of each of those years, so that the whole loss is accounted for in the 4 years. *Depreciation* is the name given to the loss in value of a fixed asset due to its being used in the business, and the amount of depreciation incurred during the year will be shown as an expense in the profit and loss account for that year. At the same time the amount of the fixed asset shown in the balance sheet at the end of the year will be reduced by the depreciation charged or written off against the profit. An alternative name for depreciation, *amortisation*, is used for assets such as leasehold property which have a predetermined life and steadily reduce in value over that time.

Methods of calculating depreciation

In practice the exact 'life' of an asset, i.e. the length of time it will be used in the business, cannot be known for certain when it is acquired, unless it is something like a lease. Nor can the amount which will be realised, if any, when it is disposed of, nor the rate at which the depreciation occurs in each year over the whole life of the asset. The result is that it is necessary to calculate a reasonable estimate of the depreciation in each year, using a method suitable to the asset and the circumstances. In accounting, providing for an expense which is known to have been incurred but of which the amount is not certain is referred to as making a *provision* for that expense, and a provision for depreciation will be made in the accounts each year.

Straight line method

This assumes that the loss is incurred evenly over the whole period, so that, if shown on a graph, it would appear as a straight line. In the case of the motor van referred to above, assume that it was bought at the beginning of year 1, and it is expected that it will be sold at the end of year 4. It will be seen that in each financial year the depreciation would be £1,000.

If the van were bought on 1 July in year 1, and the balance sheet date is 30 September, there would be 3 months' ownership in year 1, and 9 months' ownership in year 5, when it was sold. So in year 1 there would be 3/12ths of the depreciation for a full year, or £250. In each of years 2, 3, and 4 the depreciation would be £1,000, and in year 5 the depreciation would be 9/12ths of £1,000, or £750. The total depreciation still amounts to £4,000, but spread over five annual accounts because the dates of purchase and sale did not coincide with the financial year. The amounts shown in the annual accounts would be as follows:

	£
Cost	5,000
Profit and loss a/c for year to 30 Sept. year 1	250
Balance sheet as at 30 Sept. year 1	4,750
Profit and loss a/c for year to 30 Sept. year 2	1,000
Balance sheet as at 30 Sept. year 2	3,750
Profit and loss a/c for year to 30 Sept. year 3	1,000
Balance sheet as at 30 Sept. year 3	2,750
Profit and loss a/c for year to 30 Sept. year 4	1,000
Balance sheet as at 30 Sept. year 4	1,750
Profit and loss a/c for year to 30 Sept. year 5	750
	1,000
Sold for	1,000
Balance sheet as at 30 Sept. year 5	NIL

If the eventual disposal was for more (or less) than £1,000, the depreciation charged to the profit and loss account in year 5 would be adjusted by an item called 'Profit (or loss) on sale of fixed asset', or, more accurately, 'Overprovision (or underprovision) of depreciation in previous years'.

The Companies Acts 1948 to 1981 require that companies show in their balance sheets not just the balance remaining on fixed assets but also the original cost and the aggregate depreciation to date. This practice is also generally followed for all balance sheets, although there is no legal obligation to do so for businesses owned by sole traders or partnerships. In the example above, the balance sheets would look like this:

Balance sheet as at 30 September (year 1)

Fixed assets	Cost	Aggregate depn	Balance
	£	£	£
Motor vans	5,000	250	4,750

Balance sheet as at 30 September (year 2)

Fixed assets	Cost	Aggregate depn	Balance
	£	£	£
Motor vans	5,000	1,250	3,750

Balance sheet as at 30 September (year 3)

Fixed assets	Cost	Aggregate depn	Balance
	£	£	£
Motor vans	5,000	2,250	2,750

Balance sheet as at 30 September (year 4)

Fixed assets	Cost	Aggregate depn	Balance
	£	£	£
Motor vans	5,000	3,250	1,750

In year 5 the van would be sold for £1,000, and a further £750 depreciation would be written off to the profit and loss account, so there would be no entry under this heading in the balance sheet in year 5 unless a new motor van was purchased.

In order more readily to provide the information required for the balance sheet, the cost of the asset and the accumulated provision for depreciation on that asset will be recorded in separate accounts in the ledger. The cost remains unchanged from year to year, but the provision for depreciation increases as each year's depreciation charge is added, as follows:

Trial balance as at 30 September (year 1)

	Dr	Cr
	£	£
Motor vans	5,000	
Provision for depreciation on motor vans		250

Trial balance as at 30 September (year 2)

	Dr	Cr
	£	£
Motor vans	5000	
Provision for depreciation on motor vans		1,250

Trial balance as at 30 September (year 3)

	Dr £	Cr £
Motor vans	5000	
Provision for depreciation on motor vans		2,250

Trial balance as at 30 September (year 4)

	Dr £	Cr £
Motor vans	5000	
Provision for depreciation on motor vans		3,250

Trial balance as at 30 September (year 5)

	Dr £	Cr £
Motor vans	5000	
Provision for depreciation on motor vans		4,000

At the end of year 5 the balances on these two accounts and the £1,000 received on the sale of the van would be set off against one another, leaving a net nil balance.

Reducing balance method

Assets such as motor vehicles, which have a strong secondhand market, lend themselves to estimation of the future life and residual value. But some assets, such as specialised equipment, have a problematical life at the end of which they may have only scrap value or no value at all, making the straight line method difficult to estimate. In addition, it may be thought wrong in principle to assume that depreciation is evenly spread over the life of an asset. The reducing balance method covers these points by calculating the depreciation for each year as a set percentage of the balance of cost remaining at the beginning of that year:

		£
Kitchen equipment – cost year 1		3,000
Depreciation for year 1	(say 10% of £3,000)	300
Balance at end of year		2,700
Depreciation for year 2	(10% of £2,700)	270
Balance at end of year 2		2,430
Depreciation for year 3	(10% of £2,430)	243
Balance at end of year 3		2,187
Depreciation for year 4	(10% of £2,187)	219
Balance at end of year 4		1,968

and so on until the equipment is taken out of use, the balance constantly reducing but never completely disappearing.

The advantages claimed for the reducing balance method are:

1 A residual value is automatically allowed for in the calculation.
2 A higher depreciation charge is provided in earlier years when maintenance costs are low, and lower depreciation in later years when maintenance costs are high, thus averaging out the total cost of using the asset shown in each year. However, it may be thought that doing this is a misleading pretence that the cost of using the asset is the same each year, and that if an old machine is becoming too expensive to run, the accounts should show this. It is because of differing views such as these that alternative methods continue to be used, instead of one method being universally adopted.

The most common percentages used in calculating depreciation are 20 per cent or 25 per cent for motor vehicles, 10 per cent for general equipment, and 5 per cent for long-lasting plant or furniture. These figures are of course only a guide, and may be varied in particular circumstances.

Revaluation method

Some fixed assets comprise a great many very small items treated as one conglomerate item, such as cutlery, china, glassware, kitchen utensils, linen, or loose tools. Individual small items may be lost or broken and replaced during the year, and a percentage calculation may therefore be regarded as unsuitable for this particular asset. In that case a valuation would be made at the end of the year, and the difference written off to profit and loss account as depreciation.

Replacement method

This is an alternative to the revaluation method, and will be used for the same groups of small items. It assumes that once the business is established, the total value of such items will remain constant year by year. The amount shown as an asset in the balance sheet each year is left unchanged, and expenditure on replacements is written off to the profit and loss account as an expense.

Depreciation on assets bought and sold

When fixed assets are bought or sold during the year the question arises whether depreciation should be calculated for the part year, and, in the case of sales of fixed assets, what should be done about any difference between the amount realised and the written-down value (WDV) in the books. There are two main methods used for calculating depreciation in the year of purchase or sale:

1   Apportion the full year's depreciation on the basis of the number of months' ownership during the year. For this purpose fractions of months are usually ignored. So if an asset is bought or sold 5 months after the beginning of the financial year, and the full year's depreciation would have been £600, the depreciation in that year is 5/12 × £600 = £250.
2   Provision for a full year's depreciation is made for all assets owned at the end of the financial year, ignoring part years of ownership. This means that depreciation for a full year is calculated for an asset bought during the year, but no depreciation is calculated for an asset sold during the year.

In method 1 it is necessary to know the date of purchase or sale in order to calculate the apportionment, whereas in method 2 it is sufficient to know that the purchase or sale took place during the year. For examination purposes, the examiners' intentions can accordingly be recognised by whether or not the date is specified in the question.

Example 1

A restaurant which makes up its annual accounts to 31 October each year bought new kitchen equipment costing £1,500 in the year ending 31 October 19.. Depreciation was taken at 10 per cent per annum on the straight line basis, and after 4 years of use in the kitchen the equipment was sold for £850.
   Show the profit and loss account entries each year in respect of this equipment.
   Answer. On a straight line basis the charge each year for depreciation will be £150, and as no accurate dates are given for purchase and sale, there can be no apportionment. If the equipment was used for 4 years, then it was sold in the fifth year after purchase.
   Profit and loss account entries:

		£
19.. (year of purchase)	Depreciation	150
Year 2	Depreciation	150
Year 3	Depreciation	150
Year 4	Depreciation	150
Year 5	Loss on sale of fixed asset	50

Example 2

A restaurant which makes up its annual accounts to 31 October each year bought new kitchen equipment costing £1,500 on 1 July 19.. Depreciation was taken at 10 per cent per annum on the straight line basis, calculated for each month of ownership. The equipment was sold on 30 April in the fourth year after purchase for £850.
   Show the profit and loss account entries each year in respect of this equipment.
   Answer. The depreciation charge per year is £150, and in the first year would be 4/12 × £150 = £50. In the final year depreciation is charged from 1 November to 30 April and amounts to 6/12 × £150 = £75.

Profit and loss Account entries:

		£	£
19.. (year of purchase)	Depreciation		50
Year 2	Depreciation		150
Year 3	Depreciation		150
Year 4	Depreciation		150
Year 5	Depreciation	75	
	Loss on sale of fixed asset	75	150

In both the above examples the facts are the same, only the decision about how the depreciation should be allocated between the relevant years has changed. The total amount lost on this asset over the period covered by the five profit and loss accounts is the same in both cases (£1500 – £850 = £650) and the total amounts charged to profit and loss account must add up to this figure.

Profit or loss on sale

When an asset is sold, the accumulated provision for depreciation is deducted from the cost, and the resulting written-down value set against the amount realised on sale. Because the depreciation each year has been calculated on the basis of estimated asset life and residual value, it would be unusually fortunate if the WDV exactly equalled the sale price. The difference is generally referred to as profit or loss on sale, although properly speaking it is an over- or under-provision of depreciation in previous years. Whichever way it is described, it should be taken to the profit and loss account, and is best shown as an adjustment to the depreciation charge for the year.

Question

The balance sheet at 31 January 19.. showed kitchen equipment at cost £14,800, depreciation £8,700, balance £6,100. Depreciation is provided each year at 10 per cent on the straight line basis, assuming no residual value, on assets owned at the end of the year.

During the following year refrigeration equipment which had cost £1,600 5 years previously was sold for £100. Show the profit and loss account and balance sheet entries after the sale.

Answer

Working
Depreciation on equipment sold (5 years @ £160 pa) = £800

	Cost £	Depn £	Balance £
Balance sheet figures 31 Jan. 19..	14,800	8,700	6,100
Less amounts included for equipment sold	1,600	800	800
	13,200	7,900	5,300
Depreciation for year on equipment still owned (10%)		1,320	(1,320)
Balance sheet at end of year	13,200	9,220	3,980

WDV of equipment sold	800
Sold for	100
Depreciation under-provided in previous years	700

Profit and loss account for the year ended 31 January 19..

	£	£
Depreciation on kitchen equipment	1,320	
Add depreciation under-provided in previous years	700	2,020

Balance sheet as at 31 January 19..

Fixed assets	Cost £	Depn £	£
Kitchen equipment	13,200	9,220	3,980

Examination working

The method of working shown above is useful in many examination questions where it is required to reconcile the balance sheet figures at the beginning and end of the year, and not all the figures are stated in the question. The essential fact to remember is that the figures at the end of the year will consist of those at the beginning of the year plus or minus changes during the year. Changes during the year will consist of:

1   Assets disposed of will be included in the cost, aggregate depreciation, and balance figures for last year, and must be deducted.
2   New assets acquired must be added to the cost and balance figures.
3   Depreciation for the year (including depreciation on new assets acquired)

must be added to the aggregate depreciation and *deducted* from the balance figures.

Question

The net balance of fixed assets in last year's balance sheet amounted to £29,000, and at the end of this year £32,000. The original cost up to last year amounted to £48,000, and purchases of new equipment since then amounted to £10,000. Assets which had cost £2,000 4 years ago were sold for £1,000. Depreciation had been provided at 10 per cent on the straight line basis (3 years' depreciation provided up to last year on assets sold). What amounts would appear in the profit and loss account and balance sheet this year?

Answer

Working
Depreciation on equipment sold £2,000 @ 10% pa = £200 pa × 3 years = £600
WDV = cost £2,000 − depn £600 = £1,400

	Cost £	*Depn* £	*Balance* £
Balance sheet last year	48,000	19,000	29,000
Less sales (loss on sale			
£1,400 − £1,000 = £400)	2,000	600	1,400
	46,000	18,400	27,600
Additions	10,000		10,000
	56,000		37,600
Depreciation this year (10% on			
£56,000)		5,600	(5,600)
	56,000	24,000	32,000

(NB. Those figures which were not supplied in the question can be calculated because cost less depreciation equals balance.)

Profit and loss account for the year ended . . .

	£	£
Depreciation on fixed assets	5,600	
Add loss on sale of fixed assets	400	6,000

Balance sheet as at . . .

	Cost £	*Depn* £	*Balance* £
Fixed assets	56,000	24,000	32,000

Balance sheet with depreciation provisions

We have already seen that the original cost of fixed assets, and the aggregate depreciation on each asset to date, must be shown in the balance sheet in addition to the balance which is added in to the total capital employed. So far as the balance sheet is concerned, these figures are notes of how the balance is made up, and are not themselves carried forward in the balance sheet. In the ledger, however, and in the trial balance which is extracted from it, the cost and provision for depreciation are shown on separate accounts, and the balance is not shown at all. It is found only by deduction on the balance sheet.

Trial balance as at 28 February 19..

	Dr £	Cr £
Share capital – 80,000 Ordinary Shares of £1 each		80,000
General reserve		18,000
Profit and loss account		4,400
10% debentures		30,000
Freehold premises	101,600	
Furniture, fixtures and fittings	23,300	
Kitchen equipment	17,800	
Motor vehicles	8,400	
Cutlery, china and glass (at valuation)	2,700	
Provision for depreciation on freehold buildings		6,100
Provision for depreciation on furniture, F & F		6,900
Provision for depreciation on kitchen equipment		7,100
Provision for depreciation on motor vehicles		2,100
Sundry debtors and creditors	1,800	6,700
Balance at bank	3,200	
Cash floats and petty cash	400	
Food and wine stocks	2,100	
	161,300	161,300

Balance sheet as at 28 February 19..

Utilisation of capital

Fixed assets

	Cost £	Depn £	Balance £
Freehold premises	101,600	6,100	95,500
Furniture, fixtures and fittings	23,300	6,900	16,400
Kitchen equipment	17,800	7,100	10,700
Motor vehicles	8,400	2,100	6,300
Cutlery, china, glass, at valuation	2,700		2,700
	153,800	22,200	131,600

	£	£	£
Current assets			
Stock		2,100	
Debtors		1,800	
Bank balance		3,200	
Cash in hand		400	
		7,500	
Less current liabilities			
Sundry creditors		6,700	800
			132,400

Sources of capital			
Share capital – 80,000 ordinary			
shares of £1 each			80,000
Reserves			
General reserve	18,000		
Unappropriated profit	4,400		22,400
Shareholders' interest			102,400
10% debentures			30,000
			132,400

Exercises

1 What amounts would be included in the balance sheet under the headings cost, and aggregate depreciation to date, in respect of equipment purchased 5 years before for £2,200? Depreciation is provided at 10 per cent pa on the reducing balance method on all equipment owned at the end of each year.

2 The entry in an hotel's balance sheet for last year in respect of furniture and equipment was as follows:

Cost	Depreciation	Balance
£	£	£
27,100	8,800	18,300

Depreciation is provided each year at 10 per cent on the straight line basis on assets owned at the end of the year.

During the year just ended kitchen equipment which had cost £1,800 4 years ago was sold for £200, and new equipment was purchased for £2,100. Show the balance sheet entries for the year just ended.

3 The balance sheet figures for this year and last year in respect of furniture were as follows:

	Last year	*This year*
	£	£
Original cost	45,900	50,500
Aggregate depreciation	21,400	22,550
Balance	24,500	27,950

During the year furniture which had cost £5,200 had been sold for £600. Three-quarters of its useful life had been written off. New equipment costing £9,800 had been purchased.

You are required to show the entries which should appear in the profit and loss account this year.

7 Adjustments for stocks, accruals, and payments in advance

At the date of any balance sheet it is unlikely that expenses will have been paid exactly up to date. Some will be paid quarterly or monthly for the period just ended (in arrears), some for the period just starting (in advance). Some expenses, such as insurance premiums, are paid annually in advance; some, such as business rates, are paid half-yearly in advance. Even without these fixed period payments, some expenses, such as purchases of food, involve buying more than we can use up in one day, so that at the balance sheet date there are stocks left over to be used in the following period. This may be true not only of purchases of goods for resale, but also fuel oil, cleaning materials and stationery.

The result is that at the end of any accounting period there will be some expenses still owing which will be paid in the next period, and some already paid which properly relate to the next period. These should be adjusted for in preparing the accounts, and as always the adjustment will need a double entry. One entry will increase or reduce the amount of the expense shown in the profit and loss account for this year, and the other entry will show in the balance sheet as a creditor to be paid next year, or as an asset (expense already paid) which will be used up next year.

Example

PEARL RESTAURANT
Trial balance at 30 November 19..

	Dr £	Cr £
Sales		149,217
Opening stock	247	
Purchases	55,381	
Salaries and wages	34,500	
Discounts received		499
Various expenses	38,188	
5% mortgage loan		18,000
Mortgage loan interest	750	
Freehold premises at cost	118,850	
Furniture and equipment at cost	20,000	
Provision for depreciation		2,500

Bank balance	7,150	
Capital account		117,000
Drawings	12,150	
	287,216	287,216

Adjustments to be made:

1 £4,088 is owing to suppliers for purchases.
2 £786 is due from customers for private party bookings.
3 Creditors for expenses amount to £1,912.
4 Expenses paid in advance amounted to £1,150.
5 Stock at 30 November was £214.
6 Write off an additional £500 for depreciation.
7 Provide for mortgage loan interest owing.

Answer

It is not easy to remember the adjustments at the right time when preparing the accounts, so it is worthwhile making some helpful notes beforehand. This is best done on the trial balance itself, alongside the items referred to:

1	Purchases	(in debit column)	+4,088	
		(in credit column, marked Crs)		+4,088
2	Sales	(in credit column)		+786
		(in debit column, marked Drs)	+786	
3	Expenses	(in debit column)	+1,912	
		(in credit column, marked Crs)		+1,912
4	Expenses	(in debit column)	−1,150	
		(in credit column, marked Drs)	+1,150	
5	Stock	(in credit column, marked P&L)		+214
		(in debit column, marked B/S)	+214	
6	Depreciation	(in credit column)		+500
		(in debit column, marked P&L)	+500	
7	Loan interest	(in debit column)	+150	
		(in credit column, marked Crs)		+150

NOTE. Calculation of mortgage interest owing: the interest for the year is £900 (5 per cent × £18,000), so the amount owing is 900 − 750 = 150.
     When preparing the trading and profit and loss account, we must take the

figures in the trial balance plus or minus the adjustments as indicated by our notes. When preparing the balance sheet, we include the items we have marked B/S, Drs, or Crs.

PEARL RESTAURANT
Trading and profit and loss account
for the year ended 30 November 19..

	£	£
Sales		150,003
Less cost of Sales:		
Opening stock	247	
Purchases	59,469	
	59,716	
Less closing stock	214	59,502
Gross profit		90,501
Discounts received		499
		91,000
Salaries and wages	34,500	
Various expenses	39,000	
Mortgage loan interest	900	
Depreciation	500	74,900
Net profit, carried to capital account		16,100

Balance sheet as at 30 November 19..

	£	£
Fixed assets		
Freehold premises at cost		118,850
Furniture and equipment at cost	20,000	
Less depreciation to date	3,000	17,000
		135,850
Current assets		
Stock in hand	214	
Sundry debtors	786	
Payments in advance	1,100	
Cash at bank	7,150	
	9,250	
Less current liabilities		
Sundry creditors	6,150	3,100
		138,950

	£	£
Capital account as last year	117,000	
Add net profit	16,100	
	133,100	
Less drawings	12,150	120,950
Mortgage loan		18,000
		138,950

If there are any expense stocks at the end of the year, such as stocks of stationery or fuel oil, the adjustments to be made are very similar to a payment in advance. The amount of the expense to be shown in the profit and loss account will be the amount in the trial balance reduced by the stock, and the asset of expense stock(s) will be shown in the balance sheet next to stock in trade.

An adjustment which is particularly relevant to hotels is *advance booking deposits*. When a potential guest pays a deposit for a booking at some future date, the hotel holds his money as a credit balance (he is the hotel's creditor) until he takes up his reservation and the amount can be transferred to takings. Until then, this and other amounts like it will appear in the trial balance on the credit side in one amount called advance booking deposits, which will be taken into the balance sheet under the heading current liabilities.

Exercises

1   Make a list showing what adjustments (plus or minus) should be made to items in the trading and profit and loss account and/or items in the balance sheet in respect of the following:

(a) Telephone account owing £156.
(b) Takings include £50 deposit for booking after balance sheet date.
(c) Purchases include £40 deposit paid for smoked salmon not yet received.
(d) Insurance premium £240 paid for year ending 10 months after balance sheet date.
(e) Brochures and other stationery still unused valued at £45.
(f) Furniture purchased for £1,200, of which only a deposit of £120 had been paid before the balance sheet date.

2   The following balances have been extracted from the books of the Peacock Restaurant as at 31 October 19..

	Dr £	Cr £
Capital account, as last year		75,300
Fixed assets, at cost	84,800	
Provision for depreciation, as at last year		19,600
Sales		127,700
Purchases	47,700	
Opening stock	1,900	
Wages and salaries	36,100	
Sundry expenses	26,300	
Cash at bank	13,700	
Proprietor's drawings	12,100	
	222,600	222,600

You are required to prepare a trading and profit and loss account for the year ended 31 October 19.. and a balance sheet as at that date, taking into account the following adjustments:

(a) Closing stock was £1,600
(b) Debtors amounted to £1,400.
(c) Purchases owing amounted to £3,600, and expense creditors £1,200.
(d) Expenses paid in advance were £400.
(e) Depreciation £4,300 on fixed assets to be provided for.

3 The trial balance of the River Hotel at 30 April 19.. after the trading and profit and loss account had been prepared was as follows:

	Dr £	Cr £
Freehold premises at cost	40,000	
Bank loan		13,000
Cash in hand	300	
Kitchen equipment at cost	16,000	
Furniture at cost	8,000	
Stock	850	
Capital account – A. Nonimus		47,200
Bank balance	2,830	
Payments in advance	990	
Advance booking deposits		300
Provision for depreciation – kitchen equipment		4,200

	£	£
Provision for depreciation – furniture		2,500
Accrued expenses		450
Debtors and creditors	4,930	4,750
Drawings	9,800	
Net profit from profit and loss account		11,300
	83,700	83,700

You are required to prepare a balance sheet as at 30 April 19..,
indicating the amount of working capital.

8 Partnerships

A partnership exists when two or more people act together in business with a view to profit, and have not registered as a company. A partnership has no separate legal existence, each partner being individually responsible for partnership actions. A partner may be legally bound by the actions of another partner in matters which may reasonably be taken as within the scope of a partner. The significance of defining the relationship arises when there is any dispute between themselves or with other parties, and it may be vital to know whether an individual is legally bound by the actions of another individual because they are partners.

No registration is necessary, and there need be no written partnership agreement, though partners would always be wise to set out the terms governing their relationship in a formal document, in order to avoid argument later. Matters which need to be covered in their agreement would include the contribution of capital, share of profits, whether partners should be credited with interest on their capital in the business or be charged interest on their drawings, whether there should be any salaries or bonuses to partners apart from shares of profit, introduction of new partners (e.g. son of an existing partner), and what should be done about the share in the business of a partner who dies or retires. Any of these matters may be agreed verbally, and if the partners remember what they agreed without argument, a verbal agreement will be binding.

If any matter arises on which the partners do not agree, and cannot prove that they have already agreed verbally or in writing, the provisions of the Partnership Act 1890 will be binding. This provides that if there is no contrary agreement between the partners, then profits or losses shall be shared equally, there shall be no interest on capital, no interest on drawings, no partners' salaries, and interest at 5 per cent is to be allowed on partners' loans to the firm over and above their contribution of capital.

By definition there must be at least two partners to constitute a partnership, but there may not be more than twenty partners except for banking and certain professions. This upper limit is not imposed by the Partnership Act but by the Companies Act 1948, which prohibited more than twenty partners except for banking. The Companies Act 1967 later exempted certain professions from the limit. The Companies Act comes into the matter by saying that a business may be carried on by more than twenty persons acting together only if it is registered as a Company.

The Limited Partnership Act 1907 permitted one or more partners to have limited liability, provided there was at least one partner with unlimited liability, the partnership had to be registered, and the fact of the limited liability was clearly displayed. The enormous growth in popularity since then of the limited liability company as a form of business entity has meant that limited partnerships are now seldom heard of.

A sleeping partner is a partner who takes no active part in the partnership, confining his participation to providing his share of the capital, and taking his share of the profits. The term sleeping partner is merely a popular expression describing his lack of activity compared with the other partners, and has no legal significance. He still has full liability for debts of the partnership.

Goodwill in a partnership belongs to the partners, as it would belong to the proprietor(s) of any business. If the value of goodwill increases, the increase belongs to the partners in their profit-sharing ratios, and conversely if the value goes down. This is particularly relevant if there is a change in partners, when it will be necessary to determine the capitals of the partners (including their share of goodwill) at the time of the change.

From the point of view of accounting, the differences between a sole trader and a partnership are centred on the sharing of the profit, shown in the profit and loss account, and the division of the capital, shown in the balance sheet. The sharing of profit is shown in a new section of the profit and loss account, called the appropriation section. It follows straight on from the main profit and loss account, and is not separately headed.

	£	£
Net profit		40,000
Add interest on drawings (8%) – A	1,000	
– B	700	1,700
		41,700
Less interest on capital (8%) – A	6,400	
– B	800	7,200
		34,500
Less partner's salary – B		6,600
		27,900
Share of profit – A 2/3rds	18,600	
– B 1/3rd	9,300	27,900

It is apparent that the two partners are not equal participants in the business. A has invested more capital than B (eight times as much, judging by the interest on capital), but B spends more of his time than A working in the business (B is given a salary of £6,600 to compensate for this). The amount of drawings may fluctuate from year to year, and any inequality between the partners is covered by charging them with interest on the amounts they have taken. This is purely an accounting charge on paper; no money changes hands. For this example, interest has been calculated on the whole amount of drawings for half a year to allow for the drawings being spread throughout the year. Finally the remaining profit is divided between the partners in their profit-sharing ratio 2 : 1. It is likely that the business originally belonged to A, and he has taken B (perhaps a younger man) into partnership. Perhaps A no longer gives his full time to the business, so B is given a partnership salary. After these prior shares of profit, A is taking the lion's share of the remaining profits to recompense him for his greater expertise, and for having built up the business.

If the partners had contributed capital and shared profits equally, the balance sheet entries for their capital accounts might have been shown as one amount for each of them, increased by profit and reduced by drawings. As in this case their respective capital amounts are so different, they will each be split into two amounts, keeping separate the fixed capital, and calling that part of the capital which changes with the addition of profit and deduction of drawings the partners' *current accounts*:

	£	£	£
Capital accounts – Partner A		80,000	
– Partner B		10,000	90,000

Partners' current accounts	A	B	
Balances as last year	1,800	2,100	
Interest on capital	6,400	800	
Salary		6,600	
Share of profit	18,600	9,300	
	26,800	18,800	
Less drawings	(25,000)	(17,500)	
Interest on drawings	(1,000)	(700)	
	800	600	1,400
			91,400

Exercises

1 Briefly explain the following:

    (a) A sleeping partner.
    (b) Interest on drawings.
    (c) A partnership agreement.
    (d) In what proportion partnership profits should be divided.
    (e) If losses are made, how they should be divided.
    (f) A limited partner.

2 Browne and Berndt are in partnership sharing profits and losses in the proportions two thirds and one third respectively. The partnership agreement provides that before sharing profits in these proportions, the partners shall be entitled to interest on their fixed capital balances at 8 per cent pa, and Berndt shall be entitled to a partnership salary of £5,000 pa. No interest is to be charged on drawings.

    The relevant figures for the year ended 31 March 19.. were as follows:

	Dr £	Cr £
Capital balances – Browne		45,000
– Berndt		20,000
Loan from Browne @ 10% pa		10,000
Current account balances at beginning of year:		
– Browne		740
– Berndt		980
Net profit for the year		28,630
Drawings – Browne	16,500	
– Berndt	13,050	

You are required to prepare the partnership profit and loss account (appropriation section) for the year, and show the entries in the balance sheet for partners' current accounts.

3   The Royal Restaurant is owned by Needham and Grant in partnership sharing profits equally, and the trial balance at 31 January 19.. was:

	Dr £	Cr £
Fixed assets, at cost	113,800	
Provision for depreciation on fixed assets		35,800
Depreciation for the year	5,100	
Sales		154,300
Opening stocks	1,200	
Purchases	63,700	
Staff wages	40,600	
Expenses	26,500	
Bank balance	7,400	
Debtors and creditors	3,100	8,600
Capital account – Needham		41,100
Capital account – Grant		40,900
Drawings – Needham	9,900	
Drawings – Grant	9,400	
	280,700	280,700

Adjustment must be made for stocks at 31 January 19.. £1400, and for cost of staff meals £2,100 included in purchases.

Prepare the profit and loss account and balance sheet for the partnership.

9 Companies

The term 'company' is here used to mean an organisation registered with the Registrar of Companies, and subject to the Companies Acts. A company is often referred to as a 'limited company', because the terms of registration usually include limiting the liability of members for company debts, but this is not essential, and some companies are registered as unlimited companies. Once registered, or incorporated, the company receives a certificate of incorporation and is then a 'body corporate', which means that it is legally a separate entity and can enter into contracts, sue, or be sued, in its own name. In practical terms a company signs a legal document by having its company seal embossed on the document, which is then witnessed by officials of the company.

Types of company

Companies may be formed by means of:

1 A Royal Charter – a classic example of this type of company is The Hudson's Bay Company.
2 Special Act of Parliament – the Bank of England, and some authorities for protecting the coastline against sea erosion, were formed in this way.
3 Registration under the Companies Acts – by far the most common way of forming a company, it may still be of different kinds:

   (a) A Limited Company (putting Ltd after its name). The liability of each member for debts of the company is limited to the nominal amount of the shares which he holds. Once they have been fully paid, his liability ceases.
   (b) A public limited company (putting PLC after its name). For these larger companies the Companies Act 1980 required that the name should end with the words 'public limited company'.
   (c) A company limited by guarantee (putting Ltd after its name). Each member guarantees to pay a stated sum if the company goes into liquidation. This is a convenient arrangement for organisations which do not require a share capital, but wish to have the benefits of separate entity. County trusts for nature conservation may be formed in this way.
   (d) An unlimited company. Members do not have limited liability. The advantage over a partnership is that the difficulties of changing partners are overcome, such as re-registering names of owners of assets. If the

assets belong to a company, the ownership is perpetual irrespective of changes in members.

Company accounts

Just as the differences in preparing partnership accounts centred on the appropriation of profit in the profit and loss account, and the presentation of capital in the balance sheet, so will company accounts differ on the same matters. Except for certain expenses which relate only to companies, the presentation of the profit and loss account down to the net profit is the same for a given business, whatever the form of ownership. The differences occur only when showing the appropriation of the profit. Similarly the assets and business liabilities are the same in the balance sheet whatever the ownership; only the presentation of capital is different.

In addition to the expenses of any business, the profit and loss account of a company will show directors' remuneration as an expense, including all salaries, fees, and expenses paid to directors of the company. Whether a company has two shareholders or thousands, a board of directors will be elected to make day-to-day decisions on their behalf.

If there are only two shareholders, they are both likely to be directors of the company, but since the company is legally a separate entity, the two functions of the individuals must be looked at separately. As shareholders, they are owners who share the profit by way of dividends, which will be shown in the appropriation section of the profit and loss account. As directors, they are employees of the company who receive salaries and fees, which will be shown in the profit and loss account before calculating the net profit which is to be appropriated. Directors' remuneration is required to be shown separately from other employees' remuneration, but it is still an expense, not an appropriation.

Appropriation of profit

Just as with a partnership, the net profit is brought down into the appropriation section, but here the similarity ends. In a partnership all the profit is appropriated to the partners, so each year there is just the profit of that year to be dealt with. Tax on the profit is the responsibility of the individual partners, and will be treated as part of their drawings in the partnership accounts. Because a company is a separate entity, it is itself responsible for tax on its profits (corporation tax), and this will appear as an appropriation in the accounts. In a company only some of the profit will be appropriated as a dividend to be paid out straight away. As a separate entity, the company will need to retain as much profit as is prudent for financing its future activities, so some profit will be put aside to reserves for various contingencies, and the remainder will be left where it is as a balance on the profit and loss account. It follows that every year there will be a balance on profit and loss account brought forward from last year to be added to the net profit for this year.

	£	£
Net profit for the year		27,600
Corporation tax on profits of the year		7,000
Net profit for the year after tax		20,600
Add unappropriated balance from last year		7,200
		27,800
Less transfer to general reserve	5,000	
Dividend of 10%	20,000	25,000
Balance carried forward to be dealt with next year		2,800

If it is decided to write off goodwill or the preliminary expenses of forming the company, these will be appropriations of profit for the purpose and will be shown in this section of the account. The dividend in this illustration is just one amount for the year, but an established company with regular profits will often pay an interim dividend during the year on account of and in anticipation of the final profit, to be followed by a final dividend at the end of the year.

	£	£	£
Net profit for the year			239,800
Corporation tax on profits of the year			96,000
Net profit for the year after tax			143,800
Profit brought forward from last year			11,200
			155,000
Less transfer to general reserve		35,000	
Dividends paid and proposed:			
Interim dividend paid	40,000		
Final dividend proposed	70,000	110,000	145,000
Balance carried forward to next year			10,000

Balance sheet

In a company limited by shares, which means the great majority of companies, the maximum permitted owners' share capital is limited to a total specified in the memorandum of association of the company. This is known as the authorised capital (it is authorised by the memorandum), but this amount will usually be calculated to allow for future expansion, and the shares actually issued at any given time may not amount to all of this. So the balance sheet of a company will show the authorised capital (as a note, not added in with the other figures) and the issued capital:

Authorised share capital
400,000 shares of 25p each   £100,000

Issued share capital
400,000 ordinary shares of 25p each, fully paid   £100,000

Note that the shares in this illustration have a nominal value of 25p each, which is decided by the company before the shares are issued, and may be any amount. The most common denomination is £1. The nominal value is so called because the actual value to the shareholder may be very different. A £1 share out of a total shareholding of £100,000 gives the right to 1/100,000 of the total worth of the company. Past profits may have made this amount to £180,000, so each £1 share would now be worth £1.80 in company assets. The value of the share to sell to somebody else could be different again, depending on how keen a potential purchaser is.

Most shares comprising the issued capital will be ordinary shares, and fully paid by the shareholders, but they need not be either. In addition to ordinary shares the company may have preference shares (with preferential treatment as to dividends and/or return of capital in a winding-up of the company), and deferred shares (sometimes referred to as founders shares) which defer the right to dividends until everyone else has had a stated amount, but then take a lion's share. Deferred shares are not very common, but preference shares are not unusual, and are usually identified by a stated percentage dividend to which they are entitled if any dividend is to be paid at all. A dividend is a dividing of profit, so there must be a profit before a dividend can be declared by the directors. So 7 per cent cumulative preference shares entitle the holder to a dividend of 7 per cent of the nominal value of his shares before a dividend can be paid to the ordinary shareholders, and this right may be cumulative from year to year if any years pass without dividends being paid. The cumulative effect applies only to those shares which are described that way when they are issued, not to all preference shares.

Authorised share capital	£	£
100,000 ordinary shares of £1 each	100,000	
50,000 8% preference shares of £1 each	50,000	
	150,000	

Issued share capital		
50,000 ordinary shares of £1 each, fully paid	50,000	
50,000 8% preference shares of £1 each, fully paid	50,000	100,000

Reserves

Accumulated profits belong to the owners of a business, and in the case of a company this means the shareholders. The share capital is not altered, so the additional capital brought about by the profit is shown separately and described as a *reserve*. There may be several different reserves arising in different ways, and given different descriptions in the balance sheet. They will be grouped together under the general heading of revenue reserves if in the opinion of the directors they are available for distribution to the shareholders, or capital reserves if they are not available for distribution. Some profits of a company, such as the issue of shares for more than their nominal value (issued at a premium), are not allowed by the Companies Acts to be distributed, and must be kept as capital reserves; or the directors may decide that some profit such as a capital profit on the sale of fixed assets should be kept in the company as a capital reserve. In the balance sheet the reserves will be summarised, and the total added to the share capital to show the shareholders' equity, or shareholders' financial interest in the business.

	£	£	£
Share capital, authorised and issued 200,000 ordinary shares of £1 each, fully paid			200,000
Capital reserve		20,000	
Revenue reserves			
Reserve for development	15,000		
General reserve	10,000		
Unappropriated profit	2,650	27,650	47,650
Shareholders' equity			247,650

Long-term liabilities

A company borrowing money will usually execute a legal deed acknowledging the loan, and setting out details of interest payable, terms of repayment, and security offered. This deed is a *debenture*, and is referred to as an 8 per cent debenture or 10 per cent debenture, or whatever rate of interest has been agreed. The loan is a long-term liability, and will be shown as fixed rate capital in the company's balance sheet. Interest payable on the debenture is an expense of running the business, not a share of profit, and will be shown in the profit and loss account.

In some circumstances corporation tax on the profit of the year may not be payable until 21 months after the balance sheet date. This means that in the balance sheet there will still be last year's tax owing, shown as a current liability, and this year's tax, shown as a long-term liability. Consider the following:

	£	£
Sources of capital		
Share capital (authorised and issued)		
250,000 ordinary shares of £1 each, fully paid		250,000
Revenue reserves		
General reserve	20,000	
Unappropriated profit	7,418	27,418
Shareholders' equity		277,418
Long-term liabilities		
Corporation tax payable 1 January 19..	14,000	
10% debentures	50,000	64,000
		341,418

Examination question

The trial balance of the Canard Restaurant Ltd at 31 May 19.. was as follows:

	£	£
Sales		271,000
Freehold property at cost	168,000	
Equipment at cost	36,000	
Provision for depreciation – equipment		26,100
Purchases	108,000	
Stock at 1 June last year	3,800	
Wages	78,700	
Overhead expenses	51,900	
Authorised and issued £1 ordinary shares		150,000
Trade debtors and creditors	400	5,600
Cash and bank	13,800	
Unappropriated profit from last year		7,900
	460,600	460,600

You are required to prepare the trading and profit and loss account of the company for the year ended 31 May 19.. and a balance sheet as at that date, taking into account the following information:

(a) Closing stock was £5,100.
(b) Food included in stock which had been bought on credit for £300 had not been recorded in the books.
(c) The directors propose to transfer £15,000 to general reserve, and to pay a dividend of 8 per cent.
(d) Depreciation on equipment is to be provided at 10% p.a. on original cost.

Ignore taxation.

Answer

CANARD RESTAURANT LTD
Trading and profit and loss account for the year ended 31 May 19..

	£
Sales	271,000
Opening stock	3,800
Purchases (108,000 + 300)	108,300
	112,100
Less closing stock	5,100
	107,000
Gross profit	164,000

	£	£
Wages	78,700	
Overhead expenses	51,900	
Depreciation of equipment	3,600	134,200
Net profit for the year		29,800
Unappropriated profit from last year		7,900
		37,700
Transfer to general reserve	15,000	
Proposed dividend	12,000	27,000
Unappropriated profit carried forward		10,700

Balance sheet as at 31 May 19..

Application of funds

Fixed assets	Cost	Depn	Balance
	£	£	£
Freehold property	168,000		168,000
Equipment	36,000	29,700	6,300
	204,000	29,700	174,300

Current assets			
Stock		5,100	
Debtors		400	
Cash at bank and in hand		13,800	
		19,300	
Less current liabilities			
Trade creditors (5,600 + 300)	5,900		
Proposed dividend	12,000	17,900	1,400
			175,700

Sources of funds

Share capital – authorised and issued			150,000
Revenue reserves			
General reserve		15,000	
Profit and loss account		10,700	25,700
			175,700

Disclosure in the accounts

The Companies Acts require that certain items of information must be disclosed in companies' accounts, or in reports or schedules accompanying the accounts. This is for the protection of the shareholders and the public at large, and refers to the accounts which must be presented to the shareholders at the annual general meeting each year. It does not preclude accounts from being prepared in a different form or with different emphasis for internal use by the management of the company.

The published accounts of companies must show the items required by the Acts, and will not usually show other items which are not required. The result is that a published profit and loss account starts at a point somewhere between gross profit and net profit, often described as 'net trading profit', and then shows the required items leading to the net profit. An alternative method sometimes followed is to start the account with the net profit, and show the required items as a note:

X LTD

Profit and loss account for the year ended 31 May 19..

	£	£
Net profit for the year, before tax		44,100
after crediting and charging the following items:		
Income from quoted investments	1,200	
Directors' remuneration	7,300	
Depreciation of fixed assets	3,800	
Corporation tax on profits of the year		16,800
Net profit after tax		27,300
Add unappropriated profit from last year		6,900
Total available for distribution		34,200

Examination questions will expect students to know what disclosures are required in published accounts. They may be summarised as follows:

Balance sheet disclosures

1   The authorised share capital, issued share capital, liabilities and assets shall be summarised.
2   The reserves, provisions, liabilities and fixed and current assets shall be classified under suitable headings, distinguishing fixed assets from current assets and showing the methods used to arrive at the amount of fixed assets. (This means whether assets under a particular heading are at cost or at a valuation.)
3   Fixed assets must show the cost or valuation, and the aggregate amounts written off for depreciation since acquisition or valuation.
4   Amounts of trade investments, quoted investments, and unquoted investments, showing as a note the current market value of the quoted investments.
5   There shall be shown under separate headings any amounts not written off in respect of preliminary expenses or expenses in connection with the issue of shares.
6   Capital reserves, revenue reserves, and provisions other than depreciation

shall be stated under separate headings, and the source of any changes in them must be shown.

7 The amounts of bank loans and overdrafts must be separately shown, and the net amounts recommended for distribution as dividend.

8 Where a liability is secured on assets of the company, that fact must be stated.

Profit and loss account disclosures

1 Income from trade investments.
2 Income from other investments.
3 Depreciation.
4 Interest on debentures and other fixed loans.
5 Directors' emoluments of all kinds.
6 Auditors' remuneration if not fixed by the company in general meeting.

All appropriations must be shown, and tax on profits is specifically mentioned as requiring a note of the basis on which the amount is calculated. To anyone who has seen a complicated tax computation it comes as a relief to learn that this is interpreted merely as stating whether it is based on profit of the year or whether it includes any amounts for past years.

For all the above items, in both balance sheet and profit and loss account, the comparative figures for the previous year must be shown in addition to those for the current year.

Examination question

The following information relates to the Cherry Hotel Ltd:

	£
Ordinary shares, fully paid	235,000
Preference shares, fully paid	30,000
Reserves	20,665
Freehold property, at cost	326,000
Leasehold property, at cost less amortisation	61,650
Furniture and equipment, at cost less depreciation	53,400
Quoted investments, at cost	25,000
5% debenture stock	160,000
Wages and salaries	187,200
Rates and insurance	17,500
Fuel and lighting	19,830
Repairs and replacements	11,420
Depreciation charge for the year	5,510
Amortisation charge for the year	4,200
Gross profit for the year (sales £502,950)	313,250
Other expenses	28,350
Unappropriated profit from last year	20,150

Stock	23,600
Debtors	15,535
Cash and bank balances	12,860
Deposits received in advance	2,390
Trade creditors	19,500
Preference dividend paid	900
Debenture interest paid	8,000

You are required to:

(a) Prepare the profit and loss account for the year ended 31 March 19.. and the balance sheet as at that date in a form suitable for publication and showing only items required to be disclosed by the Companies Acts.
(b) Show the calculation of the starting figure in your profit and loss account, which you should call 'net trading profit'.
(c) Indicate three other items of information which might be required by the Companies Acts to be shown.

The following information should be taken into account:

(a) The authorised capital of the Cherry Hotel Ltd is 300,000 ordinary shares of £1 each and 50,000 6 per cent preference shares of £1 each.
(b) Provide for the outstanding preference dividend, and an ordinary dividend of 8 per cent.
(c) Included in salaries is £35,000 directors' remuneration.
(d) Provide for the estimated corporation tax liability of £12,000.
(e) The aggregate depreciation on furniture and equipment at the end of the year is £16,480, and the aggregate amortisation on leasehold property is £14,800.
(f) Provide for fuel and lighting charges of £930 due at 31 March 19..

Answer

(b) Calculation of net trading profit

	£	£
Gross profit		313,250
Wages and salaries (187,200 − 35,000)	152,200	
Rates and insurance	17,500	
Fuel and light (19,830 + 930)	20,760	
Repairs and replacements	11,420	
Other expenses	28,350	230,230
Net trading profit		83,020

CHERRY HOTEL LTD
(a) *Profit and Loss Account for the year ended 31 March 19..*

	£	£
Net trading profit for the year (sales £502,950)		83,020
Less directors' remuneration	35,000	
Debenture Interest	8,000	
Amortisation of leasehold property	4,200	
Depreciation of furniture and equipment	5,510	52,710
Net profit for the year, before tax		30,310
Corporation tax, based on profits of the year		12,000
		18,310
Add unappropriated profit from last year		20,150
		38,460
Preference dividend – paid	900	
– proposed	900	
	1,800	
Ordinary dividend proposed (8%)	18,800	20,600
Unappropriated profit, carried forward		17,860

(a) *Balance sheet as at 31 March 19..*

	£	£	£
Employment of capital			
Fixed assets	*Cost*	*Depn*	*Balance*
Freehold property	326,000		326,000
Leasehold property	76,450	14,800	61,650
Furniture and equipment	69,880	16,480	53,400
	472,330	31,280	441,050
Investments – quoted (market value £000)			25,000
Current assets			
Stock		23,600	
Debtors		15,535	
Cash and bank balances		12,860	
		51,995	
Less current liabilities			
Creditors (19,500+930+2,390)	22,820		
Proposed dividends	19,700	42,520	9,475
			475,525

	£	£	£
Sources of capital			
Share capital	*Authorised*	*Issued*	
Ordinary shares of £1			
each, fully paid	300,000	235,000	
6% preference shares of			
£1 each, fully paid	50,000	30,000	265,000
	350,000		
Revenue reserves			
General reserve		20,665	
Unappropriated profit		17,860	38,525
Shareholders' equity			303,525
5% debenture stock			160,000
Corporation tax payable			12,000
			475,525

(c)   Three other items required to be disclosed:

1 Comparative figures for last year.
2 Market value of quoted investments.
3 Debentures secured on assets of the company.

Exercises

1 Explain briefly what is meant by each of the following:
   (a) A reserve.
   (b) Equity shares.
   (c) A secured loan.
   (d) Authorised capital.
   (e) Profit and loss appropriation account.
   (f) Net trading profit.
2 The trial balance of the Apollo Restaurant Ltd showed the following balances at the 31 October 19..:

	Dr £	Cr £
Ordinary share capital		180,000
General reserve		18,000
Freehold property	175,000	
Furniture and fittings	33,400	
Equipment	33,700	
Provision for depreciation – furniture		6,400
Provision for depreciation – equipment		8,600
Profit and loss account, balance last year		4,900
Opening stock	1,300	
Takings		184,500

	£	£
Purchases	62,600	
Wages and salaries	48,300	
Administration expenses	33,900	
Debtors	2,800	
Creditors		5,900
Balance at bank	17,300	
	408,300	408,300

You are to prepare the company's trading and profit and loss account for the year ended 31 October 19.. and balance sheet as at that date, taking into account the following matters:

(a) The authorised share capital of the company is £180,000 ordinary shares of £1 each, all of which have been issued.
(b) Depreciation for the year must be provided at £1,600 on furniture and £2,300 on equipment.
(c) Additional expenses amounting to £200 are to be provided.
(d) £10,000 is to be transferred to general reserve, and a proposed dividend of 8 per cent is to be provided for.
(e) Stocks at 31 October 19.. amounted to £1,100.
(f) Corporation tax on profit of the year will be £11,500.

3 The following balances were extracted from the books of the Regent Hotel Ltd at 30 November 19..

	£
Opening stock of food and wine	1,700
Debtors	16,100
Directors' fees	1,000
Investment income	2,200
Ordinary shares, authorised, issued and fully paid	200,000
8% debentures	100,000
Revenue reserve	35,000
Freehold property at cost	310,000
Furniture and equipment, at cost less depreciation	53,400
Quoted investments, at cost (market value £28,800)	26,100
Wages and salaries	185,700
Rates and insurance	14,200
Heating and lighting	23,100
Maintenance and repairs	9,800
Debenture interest paid	8,000
Depreciation for the year	6,100
Takings from accommodation and meals	414,600
Purchases of food and wine	80,200
Other expenses	28,800
Unappropriated profit from last year	16,200
Advance booking deposits	1,900
Trade creditors	13,700
Cash and balance at Bank	19,400

You are required to prepare a trading and profit and loss account for the year ended 30 November 19.. and a balance sheet as at that date, taking into account the following information:

(a) Director's salary £17,000 is included in wages and salaries.
(b) Provide for extra maintenance £900 and corporation tax £24,000.
(c) Closing stock of food and wine amounted to £1,800.
(d) The aggregate depreciation on furniture and equipment at 30 November 19.. is £16,700.

10 Departmental accounts

In a business such as an hotel, consisting of several activities which should all make a profit, it is not sufficiently informative to prepare a simple trading account showing figures for the sale of meals and the service of providing accommodation all mixed together. The accounts may show that the hotel as a whole is making a profit, but not show that a part of the hotel is not profitable and is reducing the profit made by other parts. Similarly a restaurant may have several outlets, which require at least separate trading accounts to check on individual gross profits, and possibly also separate profit and loss accounts to confirm that each department is contributing to the net profit.

This could be done on separate sheets of paper, but it is neater and easier to compare the figures if they are set out side by side in columns.

Example 1

From the following information, prepare a departmental trading and profit and loss account for the year ended 31 December 19.., to show the net profit earned by each of Regal Restaurant's outlets. Comment on any matters to which you think attention should be drawn, and suggest what action should be taken.

REGAL RESTAURANT

		£
Sales	Main restaurant	122,000
	Grill room	87,000
	Snack bar	78,000
Opening stock	Main restaurant	350
	Grill room	250
	Snack bar	150
Closing stock	Main restaurant	410
	Grill room	240
	Snack bar	160
Purchases	Main restaurant	48,370
	Grill room	37,000
	Snack bar	31,190
Wages and salaries	Main restaurant	30,870
	Grill room	26,110
	Snack bar	16,100

		£
Expenses	Main restaurant	30,620
	Grill room	21,840
	Snack bar	19,570

Adjustments must be made to the figures in respect of staff meals as follows:

Main restaurant	3,170
Grill room	2,840
Snack bar	1,690

The answer to a question of this kind will require analysis paper with enough columns to provide one column for each department and one for the total. The best place to look to find out how many departments there are is sales, or takings. There may not be purchases for every department, such as the provision of accommodation in an hotel. In addition, it is useful to provide for the insertion of percentage figures. Note that the value of staff meals which is included in food cost must be deducted from there and added to the cost of wages and salaries to give the true gross profit and the true cost of employing staff.

Answer

REGAL RESTAURANT
Trading and profit and loss account for the year ended 31 December 19..

	Main %	Main £	Grill %	Grill £	Snack %	Snack £	Total %	Total £
Sales		122,000		87,000		78,000		287,000
Opening stock		350		250		150		750
Purchases		48,370		37,000		31,190		116,560
		48,720		37,250		31,340		117,310
Less closing stock		410		240		160		810
		48,310		37,010		31,180		116,500
Less staff meals		3,170		2,840		1,690		7,700
		45,140		34,170		29,490		108,800
Gross profit	63.0	76,860	60.7	52,830	62.2	48,510	62.1	178,200
Wages and salaries		30,870		26,110		16,100		73,080
Add staff meals		3,170		2,840		1,690		7,700
	27.9	34,040	33.3	28,950	22.8	17,790	28.1	80,780
Expenses	25.1	30,620	25.1	21,840	25.1	19,570	25.1	72,030
	53.0	64,660	58.4	50,790	47.9	37,360	53.2	152,810
Net profit	10.0	12,200	2.3	2,040	14.3	11,150	8.9	25,390

Comments

1 The grill room shows a low net profit % due to having both a lower gross profit % and a higher labour cost % than other departments. The reasons for this should be investigated, and any necessary action taken.
2 The expenses all appear to be 25.1 per cent, which suggests that total expenses have been allocated to departments in proportion to sales. This basis of allocation may not be appropriate for some expenses, and will distort the apparent profitability of departments.

Example 2

The following balances appear in the books of account of the North–South Hotel as at 31 December 19.. You are to prepare a trading and profit and loss account for the year ended on that date, showing clearly the departmental contributions to the general overhead expenses of the business.

NORTH–SOUTH HOTEL

		£
Stocks at 1 January 19..	Food	1,047
	Bar	801
Takings	Rooms	110,143
	Food	67,067
	Bar	19,027
Purchases	Food	30,878
	Bar	9,705
Wages and salaries	Rooms	33,609
	Food	19,121
	Bar	5,719
Rent and rates		15,660
Administration salaries and expenses		24,392
Heating and lighting		8,712
Repairs and replacements	Rooms	7,619
	Food	3,754
	Bar	1,014
Laundry and cleaning	Rooms	3,827
	Food	1,992
	Bar	560
Miscellaneous income		1,632
Depreciation		2,400
Advertising		7,923
Miscellaneous expenses		11,327

		£
The stocks at 31 December 19.. were	Food	1,513
	Bar	897

In a real business situation there would be no question of preparing the figures without looking at the percentages, but in an examination there is no time to spare on matters not asked for by the examiner, so make sure just what is asked for. The reference to departmental contributions is a way of describing figures somewhere between gross profit and net profit, when only some of the expenses are capable of allocation to individual departments.

Answer

NORTH–SOUTH HOTEL
Trading and profit and loss account for the year ended 31 December 19..

	Rooms £	Food £	Bar £	Total £
Takings	110,143	67,067	19,027	196,237
Less cost of sales:				
Stock at 1 January		1,047	801	1,848
Purchases		30,878	9,705	40,583
		31,925	10,506	42,431
Less stock at 31 December		1,513	897	2,410
		30,412	9,609	40,021
Gross profit	110,143	36,655	9,418	156,216
Less departmental expenses:				
Wages and salaries	33,609	19,121	5,719	58,449
Repairs and replacements	7,619	3,754	1,014	12,387
Laundry and cleaning	3,827	1,992	560	6,379
	45,055	24,867	7,293	77,215
Departmental contribution	65,088	11,788	2,125	79,001
Miscellaneous income				1,632
				80,633
Less general overhead expenses:				
Rent and rates				15,660
Administration salaries and expenses				24,392
Heating and lighting				8,712
Depreciation				2,400
Advertising				7,923
Miscellaneous expenses				11,327
				70,414
Net profit				10,219

If the net profit is required to be allocated to departments, then some means must be found to allocate all the expenses, and this draws attention to the difference between direct expenses and indirect expenses. Direct expenses are those which relate directly to individual departments, such as food cost, replacement of cutlery, or kitchen wages in the case of the restaurant, and housekeeping staff wages in the case of rooms. Indirect expenses are those which cannot be identified with a particular source of income, but which nevertheless form part of the total cost. They are commonly referred to as *overheads*. Some expenses such as laundry may include items of table linen and bed linen, and may thus relate to more than one department unless a little forethought is used to separate the amounts.

Exercises

1 From the following figures prepare a columnar trading account of the Peak Hotel for the year ended 31 October 19.. showing the gross profit percentage of sales earned by each department.

	£
Restaurant takings	137,400
Bar takings	86,900
Accommodation takings	168,100
Food purchases	53,200
Beers, wines and spirits purchases	42,800
Opening stocks – food	1,500
– beers, wines, spirits	2,100
Closing stocks – food	1,700
– beers, wines, spirits	1,900
Cost of staff meals not yet adjusted	3,200

2 The Opal Restaurant has three departments, Seafood, Steaks, and Snacks. The results for the year ended 31 December 19.. were as follows:

	£
Sales – Seafood	80,000
– Steaks	60,000
– Snacks	40,000
Purchases – Seafood	31,700
– Steaks	24,200
– Snacks	15,900
Opening stocks – Seafood	500
– Steaks	300
– Snacks	100
Closing stocks – Seafood	600
– Steaks	200
– Snacks	200
Wages and salaries – Seafood	21,700
– Steaks	19,300
– Snacks	12,500
Expenses – Seafood	21,200
– Steaks	15,700
– Snacks	10,800

(a) You are to prepare a departmental trading and profit and loss account for the year ended 31 December 19.. to show the net profit earned by each department and the business as a whole. No adjustment has yet been made for the cost of meals taken by staff:

> Seafood £2,300
> Steaks £2,100
> Snacks £ 900

(b) Comment on any matters to which you think attention should be drawn.

3 The following balances have been extracted from the books of the Levant Hotel Ltd at 31 December 19.. :

	Dr £	Cr £
Freehold premises at cost	188,500	
Kitchen equipment at cost	44,800	
Furniture and fittings at cost	31,100	
China, cutlery and glass at cost	2,900	
Provision for depreciation – kitchen equipment		8,960
Provision for depreciation – furniture, etc.		6,220
Opening stocks – food	1,360	
– liquor	650	
Purchases – food	39,680	
– liquor	10,700	
Bank overdraft		4,570
Advance booking deposits		870
Ordinary share capital (80,000 shares of £1 each, authorised and issued)		80,000
Takings – rooms		80,000
– meals		100,000
– bar		20,000
General reserve		10,000
Debtors and creditors	2,310	8,340
Wages and salaries	59,830	
Operating expenses	35,180	
Administration expenses	19,310	
8% debentures		110,000
Profit and loss account, balance from last year		7,360
	436,320	436,320

NOTES
1 Stocks at 31 December 19.. were food £1,040, liquor £1,350.
2 Depreciation is to be provided at 10 per cent on a straight line basis for kitchen equipment and furniture. Renewals of china, etc., have been included in operating expenses, and no depreciation of this item is required.

3 Debenture interest for the year must be provided for.
4 Operating expenses £770 must be provided for.
5 Administration expenses include £520 paid in advance.
6 The sum of £5,000 is to be transferred to general reserve.
7 A dividend of 20 per cent is to be provided.

You are required to prepare a trading and profit and loss account for the year ended 31 December 19.., and a balance sheet as at that date.

11 *Interpreting accounts*

Financial information in some detail is usually necessary before business decisions can be made, but one item of information on its own is seldom of any great value. It may be interesting to learn that a business produces a net profit of £25,000 pa, but the proprietor or prospective investor will want to know how this relates to the amount of effort put into achieving it, and how much capital was needed.

The relationship of one factor to another can be expressed in *accounting ratios*, and different types of ratios will be useful for different purposes. The manager engaged in day-to-day operational decisions will be concerned with operational facts relating to numbers of staff, numbers of customers, average costs and takings per meal. An investor will be more concerned with profitability and capital invested. But just as it is better to have a comparison of two items expressed as a ratio rather than one item on its own, so it is better still to compare similar ratios for different periods of time. In other words, it will be more useful to know the trend indicated by comparing the ratios at different dates, rather than looking only at the figures for one specific time.

Most of the more common ratios are expressed as percentages, and it is important when referring to a percentage to be clear about percentage of what? For information about profitability it is usual to mean a percentage of sales, as a yardstick of amount of business done, and so when a restaurateur says 'my gross profit last month was 63 per cent' he is likely to mean that his gross profit expressed as a percentage of sales was 63 per cent, and for items which would appear in the profit and loss account it will be assumed that the percentage relates to sales unless stated otherwise.

Almost any aspect of a business could be usefully compared with some other aspect, but some of the more common profitability ratios are the following.

Profitability ratios

Gross profit percentage of sales

GP × 100/sales is a check on the relationship between sales and the cost of sales. It will probably be about 60 per cent for meals and about 50 per cent for wines, but will vary between different businesses. What matters is the comparison between one period and another for the same business.

Labour cost percentage of sales

Labour cost × 100/sales. In a catering business labour cost will include gross wages and salaries, plus the cost of staff meals.

Expenses as percentage of sales

Expenses × 100/sales – calculated for each heading of expense and for total expenses.

Net profit percentage of sales

Net profit × 100/sales. Again this may vary widely between different businesses, but efforts should be made to maintain a constant ratio from year to year in the same business.

Net profit percentage of capital employed

Net profit × 100/capital employed. A net profit of £5,000 may show a good enough percentage of sales, but if it took £1,000,000 of assets to earn that amount, the pleasure might be somewhat diluted. This ratio draws attention to the fact if the volume of business done is too little for the amount of capital employed.

Net profit percentage of capital invested

Net profit × 100/capital invested is a proprietor's check on whether his investment was worth having. It differs from the capital employed if some of the capital has been provided elsewhere, i.e. borrowed at a fixed rate of interest.

Net profit to dividends (dividend cover)

Net profit: dividends is a comparison of the net profit with the dividends payable out of it, for example, dividend cover three times, used by potential buyers of shares in a company.

Rate of stock turn

Cost of goods sold/average stock held over the period: the answer to this calculation, e.g. twelve times pa indicates whether amounts of stock carried are changing in comparison to the amount of business done, both items being quoted on the same basis at cost.

Working capital ratio or current ratio

Current assets : current liabilities – a balance sheet ratio which checks on the liquidity (ability to pay debts) of the business.

Acid test ratio

Liquid assets : current liabilities – similar to the current ratio but is a more stringent test, since it leaves stock out of the reckoning. The argument is that if stock forms a large part of the current assets, it may take too long to realise to be available to pay debts, and the acid test is whether the liabilities are covered by debtors and cash resources.

Average collection period

Debtors/average daily credit sales – this ratio, expressed as so many days' sales owing, may not be very relevant to hotels and catering, except perhaps for party bookings or a hotel checking that its billing of guests does not become slack.

Capital gearing or leverage

Fixed rate capital : equity capital – a matter requiring consideration when seeking or providing capital for a business. Referred to as low geared if the proportion of fixed rate is low, or high geared if the proportion of fixed rate is high. The proprietors of a business making high profits will seek to borrow additional capital at a fixed rate of interest (high gearing), instead of looking for more equity capital, which would share in the high profits (low gearing). The provider of capital would have the opposite view of course.

Example (showing comparative figures for last year)

Trading and profit and loss account for the year . . .

Last year £		£	£
131,000	Sales		124,000
2,200	Opening stock	1,800	
49,500	Purchases	45,400	
51,700		47,200	
1,800	Less closing stock	1,200	
49,900	Cost of goods sold		46,000
81,100	Gross profit		78,000
25,300	Labour cost	23,400	
37,800	Expenses	36,800	
63,100			60,200
18,000	Net profit		17,800

Balance sheet

125,000	Fixed assets		128,800
	Current assets		
1,800	Stock	1,200	
900	Debtors	400	
12,800	Cash and bank	12,000	
15,500		13,600	
	Less current liabilities		
13,100	Creditors	12,400	
2,400	Working capital		1,200
127,400	Capital employed		130,000
99,400	Capital as last year		102,400
18,000	Add net profit for year		17,800
117,400			120,200
15,000	Less drawings		15,200
102,400			105,000
25,000	Loan		25,000
127,400			130,000

At first sight these accounts show a substantial drop in turnover compared with last year, and if this is in a time of inflation, it could mean an even bigger drop in the amount of business done. The ratios (last year in brackets) will indicate how well we have coped with this trend:

1 *Gross profit* % $78,000 \times 100/124,000 = 62.9\%$ (61.9%)
Despite the drop in turnover, our GP as percentage of sales is better than last year. We should not be too quick to assume that this must be good,

however. If the increased GP percentage is just the result of increasing prices, it may be the cause of the drop in turnover. The reasons for a change should be looked into, whether the apparent effect is good or bad.

2 *Labour cost %* $26,300 \times 100/124,000 = 18.9\%$ (19.3%)
Again, comparison of the ratios reveals an improvement, and if this has been achieved without a drop in standards, then it is good. But bear in mind that rash saving in costs at the expense of quality may have contributed to the drop in turnover.

3 *Expenses %* $36,800 \times 100/124,000 = 29.6\%$ (28.9%)
This percentage is slightly worse than last year, and may be merely the effect of expenses of fixed amount, e.g. rates, not reducing in proportion to turnover. Individual expenses should now be looked at.

4 *Net profit %* $17,800 \times 100/124,000 = 14.4\%$ (13.7%)
This is the net effect of gross profit less labour cost and expenses, whether in money or in percentages, so 62.9% less (18.9% + 29.6%) 48.5% = 14.4%. The ratio of profit to sales is better than last year, but since the sales are less, the amount of profit is nevertheless not so good.

5 *Rate of stock turn*   46,000/av. stock 1,500 = 31 times pa (25 times pa)
The rate here has speeded up a little, which is all to the good so long as there is never any shortage of food when it is needed. Last year the average stock was about 2 weeks' supply, and this year about 12 days'. A slowing down of the turnover of stock would have raised the question of overstocking. Carrying larger than usual stocks should be deliberate and for a reason, e.g. taking advantage of very beneficial prices for tinned goods which will keep without harm.

6 *Net profit to cap. employed* $17,800 \times 100/130,000 = 13.7\%$ (14.1%)
This ratio relates the net profit to the amount of capital being used to operate the business. In this case it is slightly down on last year, but small variations from year to year are to be expected. A change in net profit, which has already been noted, or new equipment, which would be known about, would have a temporary effect. If the reason is not apparent, an examination of the make-up of the capital employed may reveal some change which had not been noticed.

7 *Net profit to cap. invested* $17,800 \times 100/105,000 = 17.0\%$ (17.6%)
From the proprietor's point of view, this ratio offers immediate comparison with the yield he could get if he invested his capital elsewhere.

8 *Current ratio* $13,600 : 12,400 = 1.1 : 1$ (1.8 : 1)
This test of liquidity (ability to pay debts) shows that this business has very little margin for emergencies, and it would be wise to make some arrangements, e.g. overdraft facilities, in case of sudden demands.

9 *Acid test ratio* $12,400 : 12,400 = 1 : 1$ (1.2 : 1)
In this business, with a rapid stock turn, the acid test ratio does not add very much information to the current ratio. If there had been a large, slow-moving stock, this ratio could indicate insolvency when the current ratio caused no alarm.

10 *Capital gearing* $25,000 : 105,000 =$ low geared
This will be helpful if asking the bank to advance more money, as it indicates that the proprietors have themselves a large stake in the business.

These ratios are indicators, and should not be ignored. They should be followed up and investigated, and a reasonable explanation sought for any change, whether apparently good or bad, so that action can be taken to correct any faults revealed. There may be many possible explanations for a change. A drop in GP as percentage of sales could be an indication of a management fault in pricing, bad buying causing unexpected waste, theft of food or cash takings, or faulty accounting, such as wrongly valued stocks or staff meals not properly accounted for. It is axiomatic that in a real business situation this possibility of the figures themselves being wrong should be checked and eliminated before jumping to conclusions about other possibilities.

Operating ratios

For information useful to management in the daily running of the business, it will be useful to look at comparisons relating to other facts as well as profit figures:

Room occupancy %

Number of rooms occupied × 100/total number of rooms – a room occupancy of 100 per cent may be expected for a short time in the season at a seaside hotel, with much lower percentages at the beginning and end of the season. The information is not conclusive, however, because each room could have only one occupant, or it could have two or three.

Occupancy % (numbers of people)

Number of guests × 100/maximum possible number of guests. This overcomes the shortcomings of room occupancy % in judging the amount of business being done. This ratio can be used for a restaurant as well as a hotel, taking the number of covers sold as a percentage of the maximum possible. Allowing for relaying place settings.

Average length of stay

Number of guest-nights sold/total number of guests – a check on the trend of bookings which is useful in budgeting. One guest staying for 7 nights = 7 guest-nights; 7 guests staying for 1 night each also = 7 guest-nights. If 250 guest-nights are sold in a week, and there have been 50 guests in that time, the average length of stay is 5 nights.

Average spending power per customer

Total takings/number of customers – both figures taken over a period of time such as a month or a year. It is another way of saying average selling price per meal sold and, besides checking on trends, is useful for budgeting future sales.

Average number of covers per sitting

Number of covers sold in a period/number of sittings in that period – taking a sitting as being one occupancy of a table during a session, if a place can be reset after the first customer has left.

Average number of covers per session

Number of covers sold in a period/number of sessions in that period – taking a session as, for example, a lunchtime period or evening period, during each of which it may be possible to have more than one sitting.

These are no more than examples, and any number of other comparisons may be made in order to test relationships which seem relevant in particular circumstances.

Example

A restaurant sold 19,968 covers last year, and it opened in the evenings only on 6 days every week. It can accommodate forty place settings at a time, and it is possible to relay place settings once during an evening. Annual sales were £114,816.

1	Average occupancy	$19,968 \times 100/40 \times 2 \times 6 \times 52 = 80\%$	
2	Average spending power	£114,816/19,968	$= £5.75$
3	Average number of covers per session	$40 \times 2 = 80 \times 80\%$ *or* $19,968/52 \times 6$	$= 64$

Exercises

1   The following information relates to a restaurant which opens in the evenings only, 6 days per week:

Number of customers last year	41,184
Sales for the year	£267,696
Maximum number of covers per sitting (22 tables × 4)	88

Number of sittings per evening session	2
Average wages of staff per week	£1,438
Average food cost per week (including food for staff)	£2,080
Average cost of staff meals per week	£58

Calculate the following ratios:

    (a) Average occupancy percentage.
    (b) Average spending power.
    (c) Average number of covers per session.
    (d) Gross profit as percentage of sales.
    (e) Labour cost as percentage of sales.

2 The trial balance of the Ebony Restaurant at 30 November 19.. was as follows:

	Dr £	Cr £
Authorised and issued 150,000 £1 ordinary shares		150,000
Purchases	43,800	
Sales		110,700
Opening stock	3,200	
Expenses	18,200	
Wages and salaries	31,900	
Creditors		15,000
Fixed assets	158,600	
Debtors	16,000	
Cash	4,000	
	275,700	275,700

Closing stock is £2,000

Prepare a trading and profit and loss account and balance sheet, and calculate :
    (a) The working capital.
    (b) The current ratio.
    (c) The liquid ratio (acid test).
    (d) The rate of stock turnover.
    (e) The return on capital employed at the start of the year.

3 The profit and loss account of the Rex Hotel Ltd has been prepared for the year ended 28 February 19.., showing a net profit of £22,200. The balances remaining in the books were as follows:

	Dr £	Cr £
Ordinary shares of £1 each, authorised and issued		120,000
8% preference shares of £1 each, authorised and issued		45,000
7% debentures		60,000
General reserve		39,000
Unappropriated profit at 28 February 19..		6,900
Proposed ordinary dividend		12,000
Freehold premises, at cost	240,000	
Kitchen equipment, at cost	49,800	
Furniture and Fittings, at cost	24,000	
Debtors	14,790	
Balance at bank	8,490	
Creditors		14,250
Payments in advance	2,970	
Advance booking deposits		1,800
Cash in hand	900	
Provision for Depreciation		
– kitchen equipment		42,600
– furniture, etc.		7,500
Accrued expenses		4,350
Stocks at 28 February 19..	12,450	
	353,400	353,400

(a) Prepare a balance sheet as at 28 February 19..

(b) State the current ratio, and briefly explain what aspect of the business is indicated by this ratio.

(c) State the acid test ratio, and briefly explain in what circumstances this ratio is useful.

(d) State the return on capital employed, and briefly explain what this ratio indicates.

12 *Raising finance*

It has been said that the good businessman spends money on development, but the enlightened businessman spends someone else's money on development. The phrase 'raising finance' always conjures up a vision of going out into the money market and borrowing vast sums of money, and it could mean precisely that, but it is always as well to consider exactly what the additional finance is needed for, so that the best method can be chosen to suit the circumstances. It may be that cash itself is not needed, but is only a means to an end in acquiring new assets, which could be obtained under a leasing agreement without cash. Obtaining a loan in cash is not necessarily the most suitable method, and another important factor to consider will be whether the need is short-term or long-term.

Whatever the method selected, it should be carefully considered, and suitable accounts prepared to show to any third parties who might be involved. A bank manager is likely to be much more favourably disposed to a loan application if it is supported by documents such as forecast profit statements, showing adequate profitability to afford the loan, and cash budgets, showing provision for paying interest and eventual repayment of the capital.

Short-term methods

Defer payment of creditors

This immediately makes cash available for other purposes, and as an alternative to arranging a bank overdraft it offers the attraction of needing no agreement by the bank, and does not incur bank interest. But the question of losing cash discounts should be watched, as it may be more costly than the interest on an overdraft. It is suitable for a short-term emergency.

Improve credit control

This is not normally a common problem for hotels and catering, except perhaps for banqueting or outside catering. Where debts are considerable, they constitute a source of cash which can be left idle too long.

Reduce stocks carried

When considering the benefits of bulk buying, the cost of high stocks should be taken into account. Apart from the question of storage, stocks represent capital which might otherwise be available in cash.

Bank overdraft facilities

This means arranging with the bank for permission to overdraw on the current account, and should be distinguished from a bank loan, which is more suited to a long-term arrangement. The overdraft will be limited to a stated maximum amount, but interest will be charged only on the amount actually overdrawn on a day-to-day basis. The rate of interest charged will vary according to what security is offered, with a basic minimum depending on general rates in force from day to day.

Long-term methods

Hire purchase of equipment

This is a means of spreading capital expenditure over a period in order to provide the cost out of income. Payments are partly capital and partly interest, and ownership of the asset vests in the HP company until the last payment has been made, when it passes to the hirer. For tax purposes a business can claim tax allowances on the cash purchase price straight away, and also claim the interest portion of the repayments as an expense each year of the HP agreement.

The Hire Purchase Acts govern the legal position to protect both parties, and the HP company has a direct charge on the specific asset but may not repossess when one-third of the cost has been paid.

The rate of interest will be higher than it appears at first, because it is expressed as a rate per cent for the period of the agreement on the original debt, which is reduced as soon as the first monthly payment is made. The actual rate allowing for the reducing debt is known as the APR, and is now required to be quoted on every HP agreement.

Extended credit

Payment with interest added over a period of time appears to be the same as hire purchase, but differs in that legal ownership passes at once to the buyer. Again tax capital allowances can be claimed immediately, and the interest is allowable as an expense over the period.

Hiring without acquiring ownership

This is a way of obtaining the use of equipment at an agreed annual cost. It is not so much a way of raising finance as a way of doing without it, but it should be considered as an alternative when the need for extra finance is discussed. The hire charges are a business expense for tax purposes.

Leasing

This differs from hiring in that instead of hiring possibly used equipment from the owner, the client chooses new equipment from suppliers and a finance company buys it. Charges will take into account the tax capital allowances which are claimed by the finance company. The monthly leasing charges are an expense chargeable against the business profits for tax purposes. This is a popular method of providing company cars.

Sale of freehold and lease back

As its name implies, in this method freehold property is sold to a finance house for immediate cash and a long lease back to the former owner. To the finance company it is an investment producing an income from the lease rent. To the former owner it provides cash without giving up use of the property; but a new expense of the lease rent is created, and future capital appreciation of the property is lost.

Long-term loan

Possible sources of loans include:

(a) Private sources.
(b) A bank. This differs from an overdraft in that the whole of the agreed loan is made available immediately, and interest is charged on the whole amount from the beginning. Security will be required, and if the loan is made to a company, the bank will probably ask for a debenture to be drawn up.
(c) A finance company – sometimes more willing to make a loan than a bank, though the interest rate may be higher.
(d) ICFC. The Industrial and Commercial Finance Corporation was set up in 1945 by the clearing banks and the Bank of England for the express purpose of giving financial assistance to what they called Britain's smaller businesses.
(e) A building society. This is an option open to individuals, who perhaps consider buying a large house for their own occupation and to run as a guest house.
(f) An insurance company. Another option for an individual.

Extra proprietors' capital

Offering a partnership in a business, or shares in a company, will call for a share in future profits instead of a fixed rate of interest, and this may prove expensive if profits are high. A company may limit the cost of this capital by issuing preference shares for the new capital, or by issuing deferred shares to the original shareholders. In any consideration of the alternatives of obtaining loan capital or proprietors' capital, it is wise to look at the capital gearing. Consideration of gearing will always lead to opposite views between the one who needs extra capital and the prospective provider of the capital, as what is best for the one will not be the most attractive to the other. A bank may refuse to make a loan on the grounds that the gearing is too high, which means that in their view the proprietors of the business have not enough of their own money at risk in the business to make a further loan a good investment for the lender.

13 Working capital and funds flow

It is self-evident that a business must be profitable to survive, as persistent losses will drain away the capital until no business is left. The traditional annual accounts consisted of a balance sheet and a profit and loss account, which were intended to show that profits were being made, and therefore all was well. Over a period of years, however, repeated examples came to light of businesses which were very profitable but nevertheless came to grief from lack of funds. The very profitability caused expansion which needed more funding, and if this was not available, the business foundered.

The answer to this appeared to be a *cash flow statement*, which would show the sources of cash for the period being considered, the application of cash for the same period, the resultant difference applied to the cash at the beginning, and the consequent balance of cash at the end. If the flow of cash included capital spending, which would not appear in the profit and loss account, it would show among the applications of cash and draw attention to any need for extra cash resources. So disastrous did the reliance on profitability appear to have been, that there were arguments for abandoning profit and loss accounts in favour of cash flow statements, but it was soon realised that both profitability and adequate cash were needed, and companies now produce as their annual accounts a balance sheet, a profit and loss account, and a funds flow statement, a development of the cash flow statement. Consider the following:

Cash flow statement for the year ended 31 March 19..

	£	£
Sources of cash		
Profit per profit and loss account		10,800
Depreciation charged		2,360
Increase in creditors		1,160
		14,320
Application of cash		
Capital expenditure	2,400	
Tax paid	4,200	
Increase in debtors	240	6,840
Increase in cash during year		7,480
Cash balance at beginning of year		2,840
Cash balance at 31 March 19..		10,320

The main source of cash is naturally the profit made by the business, so it is usual to start with this. If all transactions were made in cash, the balance of cash might be expected to increase by just that amount, but depreciation is not paid in cash, and credit transactions mean that sales are not all received in cash and expenses are not all paid in cash, so the flow of cash will be affected by any increase or reduction in debtors and creditors. In this example the amount of depreciation £2,360 deducted in calculating the profit is added back because it has not been paid out in cash, so the cash will have increased by that much more than the net profit. The creditors have increased by £1,160, so the cash paid for expenses has been £1,160 less than the amount charged in the profit and loss account; yet again the trading has resulted in more cash coming in than the net profit. On the other hand, the debtors have increased by £240, which means that this amount of sales is owing over and above the amount due at the beginning of the year, so the cash received is that much less than the sales figure included in the calculation of net profit. In effect the business has applied £240 of its cash to finance its debtors.

The profit earned by the business will be reflected by an increase in the assets, and to the extent that it has not been used in capital expenditure it will have increased the working capital (stock + debtors + cash − creditors). Similarly, an increase in working capital will be reflected in an increase in cash except for any changes in stock, debtors, and creditors. In the above example there appears to have been no change in the stock, or the cash flow statement would have been affected. An increase in stock means a reduction in cash (it has to be paid for); a reduction in stock means an increase in cash.

This reasoning applies to all the items in the balance sheet, in that any changes since last year will have increased or reduced the cash. A cash flow statement can therefore be produced by listing the differences between last year's and this year's figures for each item.

Question 1

From the following balance sheet, prepare a cash flow statement for the year ended 31 October 19..

Balance Sheet as at 31 October 19..

Last year £		£	£
24,800	Fixed assets at cost		25,700
4,800	Less aggregate depreciation to date		7,300
20,000			18,400

£		£	£
	Current assets		
600	Stock	800	
1,100	Debtors	1,600	
1,700	Cash	2,600	
3,400		5,000	
2,500	Less current liabilities	1,800	
900			3,200
20,900			21,600
	Proprietor's capital		
20,200	Balance from last year		20,900
4,200	Net profit		4,700
24,400			25,600
3,500	Less drawings		4,000
20,900			21,600

Answer

Study of the fixed assets will show that there has been capital expenditure of £900, and £2,500 depreciation has been written off.

Cash flow statement for the year ended 31 October 19..

	£	£
Sources of cash		
Net profit		4,700
Add depreciation charged		2,500
		7,200
Application of cash		
Capital expenditure on fixed assets	900	
Drawings	4,000	
Increase in stock	200	
Increase in debtors	500	
Reduction in current liabilities	700	6,300
Net increase in cash during the year		900

In this example the net profit of £4,700 has been calculated after charging a non-cash expense (depreciation). As this has not caused any movement of cash, it is added back in the cash flow statement to show the increase in cash due to business operations, £7,200. If there had been any entries in the profit and loss account for profit or loss on sale of fixed assets, or profit or loss on sale of investments, these would also need to be adjusted as non-cash items. Profits, having been added in the profit and loss account, will be deducted from the profit in the cash flow statement, and losses will be added. In either case there will be a separate entry as one of the sources of cash in the cash flow statement for the cash received on sale of the asset.

Funds flow statements

It has been said that making a profit or loss increases or reduces the working capital of the business, and changes in any of the other items in the balance sheet will also increase or reduce the working capital. Whether this change in working capital is reflected in a change in cash depends on whether the other constituents of working capital are affected. A more sophisticated variation of the simple cash flow statement is a funds flow statement, or *statement of source and application of funds*, which groups the information in such a way as to show the movement of working capital first, and then shows the changes in the various items making up working capital. See the following example:

Funds flow statement for the year ended 31 March 19..

	£	£
Sources of funds		
Net profit for the year		25,000
Adjustments for items not causing movement of funds:		
Depreciation	4,000	
Profit on sale of investments	(1,200)	2,800
Increase in funds due to operations		27,800
Sale of investments		6,200
		34,000
Application of funds		
Purchase of fixed assets	3,000	
Drawings	14,000	
Loan repaid	10,000	27,000
Increase in working capital		7,000
Changes within working capital		
Stock reduction	(1,000)	
Debtors' increase	1,200	
Creditors' reduction	3,000	
Cash increase	3,800	7,000

Note that profit on sale of investments £1,200 has been credited to profit and loss account and must now be deducted from the net profit as it is not an item causing movement of funds. The amount received for sale of the investments is a cash item and is included as a source of funds.

A company's balance sheet will include tax and dividends in current liabilities, both of which are appropriations of profit shown in the profit and loss account after the net profit. The funds flow statement will therefore show the changes in working capital except for tax and dividends.

Question 2

The balance sheet and profit and loss account of the West Hotel are set out below. You are required to prepare a statement of sources and application of funds for the year, reconciling the reduction in working capital since last year.

WEST HOTEL
Balance sheet as at 31 December 19..

Last year £		£	19.. £
	Fixed assets		
65,000	Freehold premises		100,000
84,000	Equipment and furnishings	126,000	
(22,000)	Less depreciation to date	42,000	84,000
127,000			184,000
	Current assets		
66,000	Stock	72,000	
42,000	Debtors	48,000	
14,000	Bank	8,000	
122,000		128,000	
	Less current liabilities		
45,000	Creditors	53,000	
22,000	Taxation	31,000	
15,000	Dividend	20,000	
82,000		104,000	
40,000	Working capital		24,000
167,000	Capital employed		208,000
	Financed by		
100,000	Ordinary share capital		100,000
	Revenue reserves		
10,000	General reserve	20,000	
26,000	Profit and loss account	40,000	60,000
31,000	Deferred tax		28,000
	Loan capital		
–	10% debentures		20,000
167,000			208,000

Profit and loss account for the year ended 31 December 19..

	£	£
Net profit after charging the following items:		72,000
Directors' remuneration	29,000	
Depreciation	20,000	
Debenture interest	1,000	
Corporation tax		28,000
Profit for the year after tax		44,000
Balance from previous year		26,000
		70,000

	£	£
Transfer to general reserve	10,000	
Proposed dividend	20,000	30,000
Balance carried forward		40,000

Answer

It will be noted that:

(a) The cost of freehold premises and of equipment have increased since last year, so there must have been expenditure of funds on this.

(b) The current liabilities last year for tax £22,000 and for dividend £15,000 are not still owing, so they must have been paid during the year.

(c) The balance sheet this year shows loan capital £20,000 which did not appear last year, so the loan must have been received this year. A full year's interest has been charged in the profit and loss account, so the loan was presumably received on 1 January.

(d) The working capital except for tax and dividends is:

	£
Last year (122,000 – 45,000) =	77,000
This year (128,000 – 53,000) =	75,000
Reduction	2,000

Source and application of funds for the year ended
31 December 19..

Sources of funds	£	£
Net profit		72,000
Adjustment for item not causing movement of funds		
Depreciation		20,000
Funds generated from operations		92,000
Debentures issued		20,000
		112,000
Application of funds		
Purchase of freehold property	35,000	
Purchase of equipment	42,000	
Tax paid	22,000	
Dividend paid	15,000	114,000
Reduction in working capital (except for tax and dividends)		(2,000)
Changes in working capital		
Increase in stock	6,000	
Increase in debtors	6,000	
Increase in creditors	(8,000)	
Reduction in cash	(6,000)	(2,000)

The end of the above statement is concerned with the change in working capital, and all the signs before the figures are therefore given as they affect the working capital, i.e. plus if the effect is that the working capital is increased, minus if it is decreased. An alternative way of finishing the statement turns it into a more sophisticated cash flow statement, showing the change in working capital only in passing and ending with the change in cash:

	£	£
Reduction in working capital (except for tax and dividends)		(2,000)
Increase in stock	(6,000)	
Increase in debtors	(6,000)	
Increase in creditors	8,000	(4,000)
Reduction in cash		(6,000)

The information given is exactly the same as before, but all the signs have changed because the emphasis is now on the change in cash, so an increase in stock or debtors is a minus figure (it reduces the cash) and an increase in creditors is a plus figure.

Forecasting funds flow

Any planning for the future should take into account the financial implications of the proposed activities, and this means forecasting not only the expected profitability but also the flow of funds. If it is proposed to take steps which will increase turnover next year, it is necessary to consider whether this action will require capital expenditure, what effect it will have on working capital, and whether sufficient liquid funds will always be available at the right time. In this connection it is not only a matter of foreseeing a future need for extra cash, but in a seasonal business there may temporarily be surplus funds in the season which need investing outside the business until needed later. A forecast funds flow statement for next year will be similar in appearance to one prepared for last year, but the information will come from budget figures which will also be used for all other financial forecasts, and must be reconciled with them. This subject of working capital management will be dealt with in the next chapter, Chapter 14.

Exercises

1   Prepare a cash flow statement for the year ended 30 September 19.. from the following information:

	Last Year £	This Year £
Fixed assets, at cost	134,700	136,500
Less depreciation	27,800	37,100
	106,900	99,400
Current assets		
Stock	1,100	1,900
Debtors	1,700	1,600
Cash	3,500	13,100
	6,300	16,600
Less current liabilities	4,100	3,300
Working capital	2,200	13,300
	109,100	112,700
Capital – balance as last year	107,400	109,100
Add profit for the year	15,900	19,200
	123,300	128,300
Less drawings	14,200	15,600
	109,100	112,700

2   The balance sheet of the Bijou Hotel Ltd at 30 November 19.. is shown below, including comparative figures for the previous year.

Last Year £		£	£
	Employment of capital		
163,200	Fixed assets, at cost		175,000
14,800	Less depreciation to date		17,100
148,400			157,900
	Current assets		
1,100	Stocks	2,900	
1,800	Debtors	1,500	
2,300	Cash	3,700	
5,200		8,100	
3,600	Less current liabilities	3,000	
1,600	Working capital		5,100
150,000			163,000

£		£	£
	Sources of capital		
100,000	Share capital		100,000
8,000	General reserve	10,000	
2,000	Profit and loss account	3,000	13,000
110,000			113,000
40,000	8% debenture loans		50,000
150,000			163,000

NOTE. No dividends have been declared.

Prepare a cash flow statement for the year ended 30 November 19..

3   The Balance Sheet of Xavier Co. Ltd at 31 December 19.. is shown below, with comparative figures for the previous year:

	19..	Last year
	£	£
Fixed assets	70,200	68,500
Stock	1,100	800
Debtors	2,200	2,400
Cash	6,200	3,200
	79,700	74,900
Share capital	60,000	60,000
General reserve	7,000	5,000
Profit and loss account	3,100	2,700
Trade creditors	3,400	2,100
Taxation owing	3,200	2,600
Dividends payable	3,000	2,500
	79,700	74,900

NOTE. The cost of fixed assets at the end of last year was £84,100. During the year fixed assets costing £6,500 were purchased, and old equipment was sold for £500. This equipment had originally cost £1,200, but had been depreciated by £600 up to the end of last year.

Prepare a statement of source and application of funds for the year ended 31 December 19..

14 Working capital management

Planning the working capital is always necessary to achieve smooth running of a business, and it is particularly important when starting a new business or expanding an existing one. It is easy enough to add up the capital commitments for buying premises and equipment, but it is also easy to underestimate the extra capital needed to keep the enterprise going while the business is building up. Cash is needed to pay wages and other outgoings, and even if stock is bought on credit, the creditors will need paying in due course.

In this connection the question of cash discount must be considered. If 2½ per cent is allowed off the payment for paying 1 month earlier than you might otherwise do, this is equal to earning 30 per cent per annum. Incurring interest on a bank overdraft for that month may well be cheaper than foregoing the cash discount, apart from the improved relationship with the supplier. Consider a bill for £2,000 which could be paid less 2½ per cent after 1 month, or put off for 2 months by losing the discount.

2½ per cent discount received on £2,000	50.00
Interest charged by bank at (say) 18 per cent for 1 month	30.00
Saving by paying promptly	£20.00

This needs to be considered as a matter of planning in the knowledge of the facts applying at the time, rather than over hastily jumping to conclusions. Similarly other effects may be considered.

Questions

Consider the following balance sheet:

Balance sheet at end of year 1

	£	£
Fixed assets		100,000
Current assets		
Stock	6,000	
Debtors	11,000	
Cash	2,000	
	19,000	

	£	£
Less current liabilities	7,000	12,000
		112,000
Proprietor's capital		102,000
Loan		10,000
		112,000

(a) If all the stock is sold at cost (£6,000) and all debts collected, cash would be £19,000 instead of £2,000. Is the working capital any greater than it was?

(b) If the stock had been sold for £7,000 (i.e. at £1,000 profit), what would be the effect on working capital?

(c) If in a year profits of £26,000 are made, what is the effect on funds?

(d) If in calculating the profit we had allowed for £3,000 depreciation, what would be the effect on funds?

Answers

(a) No. The composition of working capital is different, but the total amount remains the same.

(b) The amount of working capital would be increased by the £1,000 profit.

(c) The working capital at the end of the year will be £26,000 more than at the beginning.

(d) The working capital at the end of the year would be £29,000 more than at the beginning, because the depreciation is an expense which reduces the profit but is not paid for out of funds.

Question

Prepare a forecast statement of sources and application of funds for year 2, and a forecast balance sheet at the end of year 2, taking into account the following estimates:

1 Net profit for the year is expected to be £25,000, after writing off £4,000 depreciation.

2 The value of stock held will be restricted to £5,000.

3 Estimates of the sales and purchases in the last month of the year suggest that debtors will be £12,000, and creditors £4,000.

4 Drawings for the coming year are estimated at £8,000.

5 It is planned to purchase new equipment costing £3,000, and the loan is repayable in full.

Answer

Forecast sources and application of funds statement for year 2

	£	£
Sources of funds		
Net profit		25,000
Add depreciation		4,000
		29,000
Application of funds		
Purchase of new equipment	3,000	
Drawings	8,000	
Loan repaid	10,000	21,000
Increase in working capital		8,000
Changes within working capital		
Reduction in stock	(1,000)	
Increase in debtors	1,000	
Reduction in creditors	3,000	
Increase in cash (balancing figure)	5,000	8,000

Forecast balance sheet at end of year 2

	£	£
Fixed assets (including £3,000 additions during the year)		103,000
Less depreciation		4,000
		99,000
Current assets		
Stock	5,000	
Debtors	12,000	
Cash	7,000	
	24,000	
Less current liabilities	4,000	20,000
		119,000
Proprietor's capital		
Balance last year		102,000
Add net profit for year		25,000
		127,000
Less drawings		8,000
		119,000
Loan as last year	10,000	
Less repaid	10,000	–
		119,000

Forecasting working capital requirements

Estimations of the requirements of working capital may be made from the detailed estimates of future operations, which will be the same figures used in estimating future profits. Calculations of this kind are very useful for providing a starting point in looking into the future, but they should always be looked at critically afterwards to see that they are reasonable. A pious hope that a particular result will be achieved does not make it a fact, and special care should be taken to see that any optimistic view of the future is justified by planned activities.

Question

Estimates for the Golden Restaurant forecast 30,000 covers will be sold in the coming year, and the average selling price will be £3.50. Menu prices will be calculated by adding a mark-up of 150 per cent to food cost; 90 per cent of sales are for cash, and 10 per cent on 1 month credit. The rate of stock-turn is 24 times per year. All purchases are on 1 month credit. It is desired to maintain a current ratio of 1.5:1.

Prepare a statement showing the make-up of the average working capital required, and comment on whether the desired current ratio is adequate.

Answer

GOLDEN RESTAURANT

		£
Forecast sales	$30,000 \times £3.50$	105,000
Average debtors	$1/12 \times 10\% \times £105,000$	875
Purchases	$40\% \ (100/100 + 150) \times £105,000$	42,000
Average creditors	$1/12 \times £42,000$	3,500
Average stock	$1/24 \times £42,000$	1,750
Average working capital required:		
Stock		1,750
Debtors		875
Cash (balance to make C/assets $1.5 \times £3,500$)		2,625
		5,250
Less creditors		3,500
Working capital		1,750

The current ratio of 1.5:1 is barely adequate because of the relatively high stock, which leaves the acid test ratio at 1:1. Payment of creditors will depend upon prompt collection from debtors.

Working capital cycle

This phrase is a reference to the way the different elements of working capital replace one another in the ordinary course of business: *stock* is purchased on credit, creating *creditors*; the stock is sold on credit, creating *debtors*; the debtors pay, creating *cash*; and the cash is used to pay the *creditors*. Then the whole cycle begins again.

Control of working capital

Control of the working capital available to a business is achieved by controlling its component parts – stock, debtors, cash, and creditors.

Stock

Regular checking of the rate of stock-turn will draw attention to stocks becoming out of proportion. Physical examination of stocks and keeping of stock records will detect slow-moving stocks. Above all, there should be proper planning of stock levels and consideration of what quantities should be bought.

Debtors

Care must be taken over giving credit, and over making it clear what the terms are. The system of recording credit sales should be examined to ensure that all goods and services taken by customers are properly charged. The average collection period should be regularly checked. Care should be taken over accepting cheques.

Cash

The system for handling cash should provide for immediate written records. An imprest for petty cash floats helps to keep this under control. A cash budget is invaluable in making sure that adequate cash resources will be available at all times, but should not be allowed to become disproportionately large without earning interest.

Creditors

As with debtors, the system of recording must be reliable. The payment period and taking of cash discounts should be planned and regularly checked, not left to chance.

Having ensured that each component of working capital is kept under close control, you can regulate the whole by the regular preparation of a fund flow chart for the period to come, so that there is a constant awareness of what is likely to happen.

Exercises

1 You are the proprietor of a restaurant business which you expect to make a net profit next year amounting to £19,000, after allowing for £2,000 depreciation of fixed assets. All sales are for cash, so there are no trade debtors, but expenses paid in advance next year are likely to be £300 more than this year. Creditors will be £1,000 more than this year. You require drawings for personal expenses amounting to £1,000 per month, and during the coming year capital expenditure will be needed on new kitchen equipment costing £4,000.

   Prepare a forecast statement of sources and application of funds for next year to show what difference there will be in the working capital.

   If stocks remain about the same as they are now, what will be the comparative cash position at the end of next year?

2 The assets and liabilities of an hotel at 31 October in year 1 are as follows: freehold property £175,000; furniture and equipment £29,000; stocks £1,600; trade creditors £4,900; debtors £2,300; expense creditors £700; advance booking deposits £500; bank overdraft £7,100: cash in hand £300.

   During year 2, it is expected that:
   (a) After charging wages £42,700, depreciation £3,500, and other expenses £18,900, the net profit will be £21,000.
   (b) Capital expenditure of £12,000 will be needed, and a long-term loan of £15,000 will be negotiated.
   (c) Proprietors' drawings for the year will be £15,000.

   You are to prepare a statement showing the estimated working capital at the end of year 2.

3 The Stilson Restaurant is planning that sales of meals next year will amount to 24,000 meals. A range of meals will be sold, but it is expected that the average price of meals sold will be £5.25; 90 per cent of sales are for cash, and 10 per cent are on 1 month credit. Purchases amount to 40% of sales, and are

paid for on 1 month credit. The rate of stock turn is 24 times per annum.

You are required to prepare a statement showing the make-up of the average working capital which will be required in order to maintain a current ratio of 2:1.

15 Capital investment appraisal

Decisions about capital investment such as the purchase of fixed assets are very important because of the size of the transactions, which may take years to pay for, and the fact that the earning capacity of the business may also be affected for years ahead. There will be many factors to consider in making these decisions, some of them technical and some financial, and it is useful if the financial considerations can be formalised so that valid conclusions can be drawn.

The financial considerations will come under three general headings:

1 Will the investment pay for itself? The answer must take into account the capital cost of the investment and the future income which it is expected to generate.
2 Which is best of alternative possibilities? There may be a choice of two machines costing different amounts and having different capacities, so that a direct comparison is not immediately obvious.
3 What is the best way to pay for the investment? Terms for acquiring an asset may vary between paying the whole amount immediately but at a discount, paying a deposit now and the balance at some future date, or having all payments deferred but at an extra charge.

To help in reaching a decision on these considerations there are various techniques which can be applied.

Pay-back method

The basis of this method is a calculation of how many years it will take for the cash earned from the asset to pay back the outlay. It should be emphasised that the method is concerned with cash income, so in estimating future earnings from, say, the purchase of new equipment, no depreciation should be allowed for. In connection with equipment it may be that a machine is labour-saving rather than productive, and future earnings may consist of saving costs rather than producing actual income.

This is a simple technique which is commonly used for deciding between alternative projects.

		Project A	*Project B*
		£	£
Outlay		2,800	3,700
Cash income	Year 1	1,100	1,200
	2	1,300	1,600
	3	1,600	1,800

Project A will pay back £2,400 in the first 2 years, leaving £400 still to recover, which will take 3 months of year 3, so the pay-back period will be 2¼ years. Project B will pay back £2,800 in the first 2 years, leaving £900 still to recover, which will take 6 months of year 3, so the pay-back period will be 2½ years.

The conclusion is that project A should be adopted.

The method has the one advantage of being simple, both to calculate and to understand in committee. An international conference of hoteliers has been known to applaud an assertion that a proposed new hotel project would have a pay-back period of no more than 2 years.

Its main disadvantages are:

(a) It does not take into account the total cash received over the life of the asset. In the above example, Project A may have a life of only 3 years, while Project B would go on producing an income of £1,800 for the next 10 years, which *in the long run* would make Project B preferable.

(b) It takes no account of the speed with which cash is recovered within the pay-back period, so that if one project costing £3,000 pays back £1,000 each year for 3 years, it will show the same pay-back period as another project also costing £3,000 which pays back £2,000 in year 1, and then £500 in each of the next 2 years.

Return on investment method

This method looks at the income generated by a capital project as a percentage of the capital outlay, just as the income from any other investment would be expressed. The income this time is not the cash return, so depreciation is allowed for in the calculation, and the average over the life of the project is taken.

		Project A	*Project B*
	£	£	
Outlay		2,500	3,600
Net income	Year 1	200	240
	2	250	270
	3	300	300
Average per year		250	270
Percentage return		10%	7½%

The conclusion from these figures would be that Project A should be adopted as giving the highest return.

This method is also comparatively easy to calculate, but as it uses the average income, it again does not take into account whether the bulk of the income will be received at different times.

Discounted cash flow (DCF)

This technique is more sophisticated and requires the use of discounting tables. It is based on the principle that a sum of money paid or received at some future date is not worth the same as that amount paid or received now, because of the effect of interest in the intervening period. Comparison of two projects with cash flows of the same amount but at different times is not valid unless they are both discounted at the current interest rate to their present value. The higher the rate of interest, the greater the difference between the value of a future sum of money and its present value.

Discounting tables give the present values of £1 for a range of rates and a range of years. The present value of any amount can then be found by multiplying the amount by the factor shown in the relevant part of the tables, for example, for rates of 5 per cent and 10 per cent the tables would show:

Year	5%	10%
1	0.9524	0.9091
2	0.9070	0.8264
3	0.8638	0.7513
4	0.8227	0.6830

If an alternative is a simple comparison of £1,000 now or in 2 years, the only question is whether we are paying or receiving. The benefit of receiving now instead of waiting 2 years is obvious, whereas the benefit would be in waiting 2 years if we had to pay. The fact that the values are different is obvious, but from the tables we can quantify the difference: the present value of £1,000 in 2 years time at 10 per cent is £826.40, which means that £826.40 invested now at 10 per cent pa will amount to £1,000 in 2 years' time.

If the alternatives are a little more complicated, it may not be apparent which is preferable without using the tables as, for instance, when offered kitchen equipment for an immediate payment of £6,000 or terms of £2,500 down and £1,000 each year for 4 years. The deferred terms add up to £6,500 in total, but are spread over 4 years. The tables show that the present value of the deferred terms option at 10 per cent is:

		£
£1,000 in 1 year	$0.9091 \times 1000 =$	909.10
£1,000 in 2 years	$0.8264 \times 1000 =$	826.40
£1,000 in 3 years	$0.7513 \times 1000 =$	751.30
£1,000 in 4 years	$0.6830 \times 1000 =$	683.00
		3,169.80
Add immediate payment		2,500.00
Total		5,669.80

This is a better option than paying £6,000 now, if 10 per cent is a reasonable rate of interest over the next 4 years. However, if 5 per cent is the prevailing rate for that time the conclusion would be different:

		£
£1,000 in 1 year	$0.9524 \times 1000 =$	952.40
£1,000 in 2 years	$0.9070 \times 1000 =$	907.00
£1,000 in 3 years	$0.8638 \times 1000 =$	863.80
£1,000 in 4 years	$0.8227 \times 1000 =$	822.70
		3,545.00
Add immediate payment		2,500.00
Total		6,045.90

The present value of the future payments is greater at the lower rate of interest, because the future payments have been discounted by less. This illustrates the importance of guessing the future prevailing interest rates correctly, and points out one danger of the technique. It must always be remembered that it is based on an estimated future rate of interest, and a bad guess can make a nonsense out of the most sophisticated calculation. Putting all the figures into a computer is no protection against an original faulty estimate.

Present value of cash return method

This is a DCF method for considering income-earning ability, and consists of estimating the cash return of an asset year by year over its life, listing the present values of these amounts and then comparing the total present value of returns with the cost of the asset. If they come to more than the cost, the project is worth proceeding with. Since the future income has been discounted at what is thought to be a current rate of interest, so long as the present value equals the cost it follows that it is producing enough cash to pay for its own cost plus a reasonable rate of interest.

Question

A fast-food company is considering the purchase of new equipment costing £100,000, which will be productive for 4 years and then be sold off for £10,000.

During its 4-year life it will earn a net cash income of £30,000 per year. If the current rate of interest for the next 4 years is estimated to average 10 per cent pa, is the project financially worthwhile?

Answer

			Present value of cash return
			£
Income – Year	1	$30,000 \times 0.9091$	27,273
	2	$30,000 \times 0.8264$	24,792
	3	$30,000 \times 0.7513$	22,539
	4	$30,000 \times 0.6830$	20,490
			95,094
Cash on sale	4	$10,000 \times 0.6830$	6,830
			101,924

Conclusion. Buy, because the equipment will earn a better income than investing the money in interest-bearing securities. However, this will only be true if the equipment can be sold at the end of the 4 years as expected, and provided interest is no more than 10 per cent.

Discounted yield (internal rate of return)

This is a development of the present value method which considers at what rate of interest the present value of the total income from the project will exactly equal the cost. It entails an element of trial and error, calculating first at one rate and then another until the required rate is found.

In the question about the fast-food equipment, it was found that the present value of the income discounted at 10 per cent was slightly more than the cost, which means that the IRR should be slightly more than 10 per cent. We will therefore try a higher rate, say 15 per cent.

There is a rough and ready way of calculating where the true internal rate falls between two trial guesses. It consists of adding to the lower guessed rate a proportion of the difference between the two rates, the proportion being related to the amounts of the discounted yield over and under the outlay:

	£
Income discounted @ 10% (as above)	101,924
Outlay	(100,000)
	1,924

Income discounted @ 15%

			£
Income – Year	1	30,000 × 0.8696	26,088
	2	30,000 × 0.7561	22,683
	3	30,000 × 0.6575	19,725
	4	30,000 × 0.5718	17,154
Cash on sale	4	10,000 × 0.5718	5,718
			91,368
Outlay			(100,000)
			(8,632)

One rate gives a discounted return £1,924 more than the outlay, and the other £8,632 less than the outlay. The difference between the two results is £10,556 (1,924 + 8,632) so the IRR will be:

Lower rate (10%) + 1,924/10,556 × difference in rates 5% (15% − 10%)
= 10% + 0.91%
= nearly 11%

We now know the required rate is about 11 per cent. Checking the figures at this rate gives us a present value of £99,659, which is almost exactly the amount of the cost. So 11 per cent represents the *internal rate of return* generated by the project, for comparison with other investments.

Using more than one technique

When making decisions about an expensive project, it will be natural to consider every possible aspect, and so it will be sensible to use more than one of these capital investment appraisal techniques in checking the available facts. Sometimes one technique will suggest a different conclusion from another, which will mean weighing up the pros and cons between the two. If, on the other hand, each test points to the same conclusion, there is a strong argument for believing the guidance received.

Question

The Directors of Bloggs Ltd are considering two investment opportunities, each of which will cost £10,000 and have a life of 4 years. There are sufficient funds to finance only one of these opportunities.

The company provides depreciation on the straight line method, and has prepared forecasts of profit after depreciation for each project as follows:

Year	Project A Profit £	Project B Profit £
1	800	2,500
2	1,000	2,000
3	1,800	700
4	2,400	400

(a) You are required to assess each of these projects using the following methods:

    (i) average return on capital;
    (ii) pay-back period; and
    (iii) net present value, using 10 per cent as the discount factor.
        (tables provided).
(b) State the advantages and disadvantages of each of the above methods.

Answer
  (a)

		Project A	Project B
(i)	Average net profit	£1,500	£1,400
	Return on capital	15%	14%

    From this point of view (A) is better.

  (ii) Depreciation is £10,000/4 = £2, 500 pa

		£	£
Cash return – Year	1	3,300	5,000
	2	3,500	4,500
	3	4,300	3,200
	4	4,900	2,900
Pay-back period		2.7 years	2.2 years

    From this point of view (B) is better.

(iii)

		Present value £	Present value £
Investment		(10,000)	(10,000)
Cash return – Year	1 × 0.9091	3,000	4,546
	2 × 0.8264	2,892	3,719
	3 × 0.7513	3,231	2,404
	4 × 0.6830	3,347	1,981
		2,470	2,650

Both projects have discounted cash returns far greater than the original cost, so both are good investments, but Project B is slightly better.

  (b) Methods (i) and (ii) both have the one advantage of being simple to calculate and to appreciate. The average return method has the disadvantage of not taking into account the speed of return, and the pay-back method does not take into account the earnings after the pay-back period has ended.

Method (iii) overcomes these disadvantages, but is more complicated, and depends on the correct estimation of an appropriate discount rate.

Exercises

1   Two alternative capital investments are being considered, and you are asked to calculate for each of them (a) the pay-back period, and (b) the return on capital invested, and comment on which project appears to be preferred.

Project A will cost £15,000, which will be depreciated at £1,000 pa. It is expected to produce a net return after depreciation of £5,000 in the first year, £6,000 in year 2, and £7,000 in year 3.

Project B will cost £18,000, which will be depreciated at £2,000 pa. It is expected to produce a net return after depreciation of £6,000 in the first year, £8,000 in year 2, and £9,000 in year 3.

2   Two alternative projects will cost the same capital outlay, but Project A will produce cash inflows of £2,000 after 1 year, £3,000 at the end of the second year, and no further return. Project B will produce £1,000 pa for 5 years and £896 at the end of year 6.

If the cost of capital is 10 per cent pa, which is the better project to invest in? If the prevailing interest rates prove to be more or less than 10 per cent, how will it affect your conclusion?

Present value table at 10%

Year	1	0.9091
	2	0.8264
	3	0.7513
	4	0.6830
	5	0.6209
	6	0.5645

3   A company is considering investing in a new project which will cost £20,000. Its useful life will be 4 years, at the end of which its value will be nil. Estimated cash returns will be £8,000 each year for the 4 years, and depreciation will be provided on a straight line basis. The cost of capital during the period is estimated at 15 per cent.

You are required to evaluate the proposal by means of (a) pay-back, (b) return on capital invested, (c) internal rate of return, and (d) net present value.

16 Elements of cost and sales

The sales of a business must be sufficient to cover all the costs of running the business and still leave an adequate profit, so the amount of sales must be equal to the total of costs plus profit. This basic equation is true whatever the amount of profit made. Even if the concern is not intended to be a profit-making business, such as a works canteen, the amounts charged must cover those costs which are not expected to be subsidised by the management, so the catering sales must still be equal to the total of catering costs plus a profit of nil, or a negative profit (loss) of predetermined amount. The important thing as far as costing is concerned is that the result should be foreseeable.

To be certain that the profit remaining will be the amount expected, it will be necessary that all sales will cover all the costs and whatever profit is required, and every sale must cover its proportion of the total. In a restaurant each dish to be served must be priced at a level calculated to cover costs and the required profit, so that the total of sales at the end of the year will give this result. In practice, after calculating the prices which would be necessary to achieve a uniform profitability, individual dish prices may be varied from the calculated figures for various reasons. What seems a reasonable charge may be affected by the factors of supply and demand, by prestige considerations, or by simple comparison with competitors' prices; but if it is known what price would give a certain result, any variation will be made knowing the consequences, and can be compensated for.

It would be impracticable to estimate the amount of every item of cost relating to every dish, but it is quite feasible to estimate the proportion of total costs to sales, and the proportion of the required net profit to sales. Examination of our budget figures for the coming year will reveal these percentages (percentages *are* proportions), and the expected gross profit percentage which will cover total costs plus net profit.

The elements of cost (the headings into which total costs can be divided) are food cost, labour cost, and overheads, using the term overheads to mean all other expenses. The elements of sales are the elements of cost plus net profit. From these premises certain equations can be formulated, and these equations will be of great assistance in calculating financial objectives from incomplete information:

Gross profit = sales − food cost
Gross profit percentage of sales (GP%) = 100% − food cost%
Gross profit = labour cost + overheads + net profit
GP% = labour cost% + overheads% + net profit%

Since food cost and gross profit together must add up to 100 per cent of sales (by definition gross profit is sales − food cost), it follows that the food cost amount must be divided by what is left out of 100 per cent after deducting the gross profit percentage. If it is estimated that a gross profit of 65 per cent is required to cover labour cost, overheads, and net profit, then food cost must be 35 per cent of sales. The amount of food cost can be exactly calculated by pricing all the ingredients used, and from this the required selling price to give a 65 per cent gross profit can be found from the following formula:

$$\text{Calculated selling price} = \frac{\text{food cost} \times 100}{35}$$

If the required gross profit is to be 62 per cent, the food cost must be 38 per cent, and the formula will be:

$$\text{Calculated selling price} = \frac{\text{food cost} \times 100}{38}$$

Note that in listing the cost of ingredients for a dish it will be a case of starting with a list of ingredients for making a convenient number of portions, and then dividing the cost arrived at to find the food cost per portion.

Question

Costings of a dish show that ingredients' cost per portion will be £2.17. (a) What price would need to be charged to the customer in order to achieve a gross profit of 63 per cent? (b) What GP% will be achieved if the dish is sold for £6.00 per portion?

Answer

(a) $\text{Selling price} = \dfrac{£2.17 \times 100}{37} = £5.865$

(b) $\text{GP\% for SP £6.00} = \dfrac{(6.00 - 2.17)\ 3.83 \times 100}{6.00} = 63.8\%$

Changes in food cost

In times of rising prices it is frequently found that a dish costing is out of date, and a revision of the selling price will be necessary if the same degree of profit is to be achieved. If the ingredients had been calculated to cost £1.90, and it was required to make a gross profit of 60 per cent, the calculated selling price would be £4.75. If the menu price had been fixed at that, and after a time the food cost increased to £2.14 per portion, it can be seen that the gross profit now being achieved is only 54.9 per cent. It is tempting to think that the gross profit is 5.1 per cent less than it should be, but this prompts the question 5.1 per cent of what? It must be remembered that percentages are not absolute numbers, but *expressions of proportion* related to sales, and if the selling price needs increasing, the percentages must be percentages of the new selling price. It is no use trying to make an adjustment of 5.1 per cent on the old selling price. Instead of trying to alter the previous figures, the full formula should be set out, using the new food cost to find the new selling price:

$$\text{New selling price} = \frac{£2.14 \times 100}{40} = £5.35$$

Mark-up

The mark-up is the percentage by which the food cost is to be marked up to set the selling-price. It is the percentage of food cost which is to be added to food cost, and since it is the difference between food cost and selling price, in amount it is the same as gross profit, but is expressed as a percentage of food cost instead of a percentage of sales. It is merely a convenience in thinking of the calculation as being a percentage of the known food cost instead of being based on the unknown selling price. We have already seen that to achieve a gross profit of 60 per cent the selling price needs to be

$$\frac{\text{food cost} \times 100}{40}$$

As a calculation of selling price this formula is cumbersome, and the same result can be found by expressing the selling price as food cost + 150% of food cost.

Gross profit is what is left out of sales when food cost has been allowed for, so gross profit is always less than sales and GP% must therefore be less than 100 per cent of sales. Mark-up, however, can very well be more than the materials cost, and in the catering industry it usually is; so the mark-up will be more than 100 per cent of food cost.

Question

What mark-up is required in order to achieve a gross profit of 65 per cent?

Answer

If the gross profit is 65%, then the food cost is 35 per cent. The required mark-up will be 65 as a percentage of 35

$$= \frac{65 \times 100}{35} = 185.7\% \text{ of food cost}$$

Menu price

The calculated selling price arrived at by increasing ingredient cost by a constant percentage may be satisfactory for inclusion in the menu. However, it should be taken only as a guide to what figure will give a calculated result, and any other relevant factors should also be considered. Such matters as comparison with competitors' prices, dishes requiring more or less labour cost than usual, or simply adjusting an exactly calculated figure to the nearest round figure may all result in a menu price which does not give the generally aimed-for percentage.

Fixed and variable costs

Many costs do not vary if more or less business is done, and these are known as *fixed costs*. Such items as rent, insurance, depreciation, and mortgage interest, are fixed in amount irrespective of how much business is done, and the proportion to be taken into account in our figures will be related to time rather than a percentage of sales.

Even variable costs may not all vary in direct proportion to sales, but may go up when sales increase beyond a certain level, and then remain static. The cost of one extra member of staff, for instance, will cope with quite a lot of extra business before it becomes necessary to take on extra staff. Some costs will vary in proportion to sales once a certain level has been reached, but will have a minimum amount which must be paid however little business is done, so that at a very low level of business they are in effect fixed costs. Again staff costs are an example of this, as some staff will be needed however few the customers. This consideration of the behaviour of costs is most important when we come to think of budgeting and marginal costing.

Sales volume

The reliance for the purpose of our costing figures on costs and profit being accepted percentages of sales is dependent on a given volume of sales. The effect of fixed costs not varying when sales go up or down is to alter the percentage of total costs to sales if the sales volume itself materially changes. If the sales volume is low, it may be that total costs will not be covered, however much care is taken in controlling those costs which do vary. If sales are very high, on the other hand, the proportionate effect of fixed costs will be less and the net profit achieved will be a higher percentage of sales, although the variable costs are maintained at a constant percentage. So any calculations of costs being a certain percentage of sales must be related to an accepted volume of sales.

Sales mix

The expression *sales mix* refers to the composition of total sales, when these comprise items of different kinds, e.g.

	%
Food sales	78
Beverage	20
Other	2
	100

The different kinds of sales produce different proportionate profits, so that an increase or reduction in *one kind* of sales will not produce a proportionate alteration in total profit.

In an hotel total takings may include food and beverage sales, accommodation charges, bar sales, and other takings. Food sales may comprise residents' meals and chance meals, which may be priced differently. Table d'hôte meals may be priced differently from à la carte meals. All these differences will have their effect on the profit percentage of total sales, and must be borne in mind particularly when forecasting future results.

Representative customer

To say that the representative customer spends £5.50 is another way of saying that £5.50 is the average selling price of dishes sold. It is a useful factor in estimating future sales, when combined with an estimate of how many dishes will be sold.

Banquets and party bookings

Costing for a banquet or special party is essentially no different from a dish costing, but, as it is a much larger unit, it may be possible to establish the actual costs to a greater extent, leaving less to be estimated as a percentage of sales. Costs of direct labour, and direct expenses such as menus, floral decorations, band hire, etc., can be allowed for with reasonable accuracy.

Example

A price is required for the annual dinner of a local society, and the menu selected will give a food cost of £414 for 120 persons. Labour cost for the event will be £224, and direct expenses will amount to £115. It is necessary to allow for general overheads at 20 per cent of sales, and net profit of 10 per cent of sales.

For this kind of problem it is best to set out the elements of sales in two columns of money amounts and percentages, bearing in mind that total sales will be 100 per cent:

Annual dinner for 120 persons

	£	%
Food cost	414.00	
Direct labour	224.00	
Direct expenses	115.00	
Overheads		20.0
Net profit		10.0
		100.0

It will be seen that the unknown expenses and net profit together make up 30 per cent of sales, so the known expenses must add up to 70 per cent of sales. These amount to £753, so sales can be calculated as

$$\frac{£753 \times 100}{70} = £1,075.71$$

or £8.96 per cover.

The rest of the figures can now be filled in, and the banqueting manager will keep the record on his files:

Woodworking Society annual dinner 25/11/19..
120 persons

	£	%
Food cost	414.00	38.5
Direct labour	224.00	20.8
Direct expenses	115.00	10.7
	753.00	70.0
Overheads	215.14	20.0
Net profit	107.57	10.0
Total charge	1,075.71	100.0

Because of the direct labour and expenses which are known in this case, it is not necessary to use the GP% as part of the calculations as we do in dish costing. However, it is useful to check on the GP% for comparison with that obtained from normal service. In this case it is 61.5 per cent, and this may be regarded as a normal margin return, a term used to denote the rate of gross profit being achieved. A special function like this may quite reasonably produce a high margin return or a low margin return when compared with normal service, depending on the circumstances.

High margin return

A high margin return may result from:

1 The food cost for a given number of covers may be less than normal because knowing in advance what dishes are to be served, how many dishes are to be served, and service in a short space of time, all contribute to reducing waste.
2 Labour cost and overheads may be higher than normal as a result of giving better-than-usual service at a function of this kind, so that the gross profit needs to be proportionately higher.

Low margin return

A low margin return may result from:

1 Food cost may be higher than normal, owing to inclusion of expensive dishes. If the selling price is nevertheless calculated to produce a normal net profit percentage, then the unusually high food cost will be an unusually high percentage of sales, and the GP% correspondingly low.
2 Concentration of service into a shorter time than would be necessary for chance trade may result in labour cost being comparatively low. The GP% needed to cover the labour cost would therefore be correspondingly lower.
3 The cost of many overheads such as heating and lighting will be less for a function taking place within a limited time than for the same number of meals spread over a longer period.

One other reason for a low margin return, which is not directly related to special party catering, is the purchasing of pre-prepared food. This means that the initial food cost is higher in order to save on other costs in preparation, and the gross profit percentage of the selling price will therefore be less.

Exercises

1 A banquet is to be prepared for 110 covers, for which the food cost will be £442.50. Direct labour cost will be £318.20, and direct expenses £146.80. Overheads must be allowed for at 15 per cent of sales, and it is required to make a net profit of 10 per cent of sales.

What charge per cover should be made?
2 You have been asked to quote a charge per head for the annual dinner of the Old Borstalians to be held on 8th June 19..

There will be 150 covers, and for the menu chosen the food

cost will be £7.20 per cover. Labour cost relating to the dinner will be £429.75, and expenses amounting to £69.75 will be incurred. In addition, general overheads must be allowed for at 20 per cent of sales.

Prepare a statement showing the costs, profit, and charge per cover in order to make a net profit of 15 per cent of sales.

3   A new restaurant is to be opened, and costs for the coming year to 30th April 19.. have been estimated as follows:

	£
Food cost	66,300
Labour cost	50,900
Rent and rates	13,800
Insurances	1,200
Light and heat	4,800
Advertising	600
Printing and stationery	700
Depreciation	1,500
Other costs	10,200

(a) Prepare a statement for the coming year showing the estimated sales, costs, and profit, if a net profit of £20,000 is to be made.

(b) Menu prices are to be calculated to give a profit proportionate to the above, and you are required to show what price should be charged for one serving of *sole meunière* if the food cost per portion is £2.49.

17 *Hotels*

Hotels generally comprise at least two businesses being run together – catering and supplying accommodation – and accounting for each aspect separately is not always easy; but unless the takings and costs of each operation are kept separate, it is impossible to be sure that each is profitable and pulling its weight. Inclusive terms to hotel guests mean that takings are mixed, and costs are often just as difficult to separate. Similarly bar sales are another revenue-earning venture which should cover the costs of providing this service to guests, including a reasonable proportion of hotel overheads.

Unless some attempt is made to split the inclusive charges to guests, it is useless to make any calculation of gross profit. The sales will include accommodation charges which have no relation to the cost of food, so the result of deducting food cost from total takings has no meaning, and is certainly not gross profit. Such a result will be affected by the sales mix, and show different percentages for no other reason than a sales mix change. So if the inclusive charges are to be split into meal sales and accommodation charges, the best way to go about it is probably to start with working out how much is the charge for meals.

This may be calculated from the food cost in much the same way as for a restaurant. The average ingredients for a normal cycle of menus should be costed, and a selling price calculated from this, using a mark-up which will cover the other costs relating to meals as distinct from accommodation. If this is done for each meal (breakfast, lunch, dinner), the meal content of any combination of charges such as bed and breakfast; dinner, bed and breakfast; or full board; can be calculated.

This raises the question of what mark-up will cover the other costs relating to meals, and allocation of hotel costs will be dealt with later. In the meantime it is possible to make a starting point from reasonable assumptions, which can be checked against actual results later, and revised if necessary. In any catering business the gross profit required to cover labour cost, overheads and net profit is likely to be about 60 per cent of the selling price. If this is taken as a starting point, an assumption can then be made about reasonable selling prices, in order to see whether these would be in proportion with the known food costs.

Calculation of charge for meals

Suppose the average food cost for breakfast is £1.84, for lunch £3.46, and for dinner £5.71. Selling prices are not known, but it is thought that lunch of the kind served would be charged at about £7.85 in a restaurant, and dinner £14.65.

A charge for breakfast can only be guessed, but if the ratios for lunch and dinner can be determined, then breakfast can be calculated on the same basis.

Lunch – if food cost is £3.46 and the charge is £7.85, then the gross profit is 56 per cent.

Dinner – if food cost is £5.71 and the charge is £14.65, then the gross profit is 61 per cent.

There is a discrepancy here, but on consideration it may be thought that a higher charge of £8.45 for lunch and a lower charge of £13.95 for dinner would not be unreasonable, and these would both give a gross profit of approximately 59 per cent. Using this percentage on the food cost for breakfast would give a charge of £4.49, which again may not appear unreasonable.

Now that a starting point has been found, it can be used as a basis to work on. Certain assumptions have had to be made, but they have been seen to be reasonable assumptions, and the resultant scale of meal charges will be more realistic and accurately related to costs than an arbitrary decision would have been. In addition, a rate of gross profit has been established, and this rate may be compared with actual results over a period of time.

Apportionment of inclusive terms

Inclusive terms for an hotel are £33.00 per person per day for full board. Selling prices for meals have been calculated at £3.75 for breakfast, £6.75 for lunch, and £11.25 for dinner. How should the inclusive terms be apportioned between accommodation and food?

	£	£
Inclusive terms to guest		33.00
Less charges for meals		
Breakfast	3.75	
Lunch	6.75	
Dinner	11.25	21.75
Charge for accommodation		11.25

In this example the inclusive charge of £33.00 may be split between food takings of £21.75 and accommodation takings of £11.25. Terms for bed and breakfast can be calculated on the same basis at £15.00 (11.25 + £3.75), and for dinner, bed and breakfast at £26.25 (£11.25 + £3.75 + £11.25).

The split of the inclusive terms can be recorded in the books of the hotel from the beginning, by having columns in the tabular ledger for accommodation and for meals (or in a small hotel with no tabular ledger, in a cash received book). Otherwise the total meal sales for a week or a month can be calculated and deducted from the total sales to find the split between meal sales and accommodation charges.

Sleeper-nights

This term is used to make allowance for the fact that different visitors will have different lengths of stay, so that any calculation 'per visitor' must be adjusted to 'per visitor per night', which is shortened to 'per sleeper-night'. In this sense one visitor who stays for 6 nights will constitute 6 sleeper-nights. Two visitors who stay for 3 nights each will also constitute 6 sleeper-nights. Two visitors who stay for a full week will constitute 14 sleeper-nights. Sometimes the term 'bed-night' is used instead of sleeper-night.

Example

In one week seven visitors stayed one night each for bed and breakfast, three visitors stayed two nights each for bed and breakfast, and forty visitors stayed seven nights each for full board. If the selling price of breakfast is £3.00, and full meals £18.00 per day, then the takings for food in the week will be £3.00 multiplied by the number of bed and breakfast sleeper-nights, plus £18.00 multiplied by the number of full board sleeper-nights:

$$
\begin{array}{lrr}
\text{B \& B sleeper-nights } 7 \times 1 \text{ plus } 3 \times 2 = & 13 \times \ £3.00 = & 39.00 \\
\text{F/bd sleeper nights } 40 \times 7 & = 280 \times £18.00 = & 5{,}040.00 \\
\hline
\text{Total food sales for the week} & & £5{,}079.00 \\
\hline
\end{array}
$$

Occupancy

When considering the income of an hotel, one important factor is the rate of occupancy, expressed as a percentage of full occupancy, which is the maximum number of sleeper-nights possible for the hotel to accommodate in a given period. Thus an hotel may have fifty bedrooms capable of accommodating ninety guests each night. For one week full occupancy would be 630 sleeper-nights. If in one week the hotel has forty of its rooms occupied by seventy guests for the whole week, and fourteen guests stay 1 night each in the other ten rooms (some are double rooms), then the actual occupancy is $70 \times 7 + 14 = 504$ sleeper-nights. This expressed as a percentage of full occupancy (630 sleeper-nights) gives an occupancy rate of 80 per cent for the week.

It should be remembered that it is possible to have 100 per cent *room occupancy* and yet not have full occupancy in terms of sleeper-nights, if every room is not *fully* occupied. Hence the need for using sleeper-nights instead of the number of rooms in the calculation.

Hotel costs

As well as apportioning the takings, it is necessary to apportion the costs of an hotel if the profitability of each department is to be checked. Food cost relates to food sales, but it will also be necessary to find out how much of the labour cost and expenses relate to each activity.

In allocating the costs to appropriate sources of income, the direct costs are easily recognised and dealt with. Restaurant purchases and bar purchases can be analysed separately and related to the correct source of income. When goods are purchased for one source but sold in another, e.g. brandy included in bar purchases but used for cooking, it is a simple matter to record such transfers daily and adjust the figures accordingly.

Wages of kitchen and restaurant staff can be allocated to the restaurant. Bar staff, housekeepers, and chambermaids can all be directly related to appropriate sources of income (they represent *direct labour cost*) and their wages can be allocated accordingly. When all these wages have been allocated, there will remain some wages and salaries for staff who are concerned with the hotel as a whole. These will include management, office staff, maintenance staff, porters, reception, etc., and the wages or salaries of all these (*indirect labour cost*) will need apportioning in some way. Similarly some expenses can be directly identified with the restaurant, bar, or accommodation (*direct expenses*), while other expenses relate in a general way to all three sources of income (*indirect expenses*) and need apportioning.

Methods of apportionment

The first method of apportionment which suggests itself is a division in proportion to sales, which has the merit of simplicity and is widely used in other trades, such as departmental stores. It presupposes that each department earns the same rate of gross profit, and incurs the same cost per £ of income.

This is unfortunately not true in an hotel, where the incidence of duty on bar stocks and cigarettes inflates the amount of takings without increasing the value. The gross profit on sales of cigarettes will be about 8 per cent of takings, on wines about 50 per cent of takings, on meals about 60 per cent of takings, and on accommodation 100 per cent of takings. It is apparent that the gross profit out of which expenses must be met is nothing like in proportion to the takings of each department.

Similarly a method based on direct labour cost is suitable for some kinds of labour-intensive business, but does not suit the circumstances of a hotel.

Apportionment on basis of floor area

The method most commonly adopted for hotels is apportionment on the basis of floor area, with a weighting where this is thought to be appropriate. The method means that costs will be allocated in proportion to the amount of hotel being used for each revenue-earning activity, and by weighting the areas it is possible to allow for some areas to be more costly than others.

The floor areas will be those used exclusively for the purpose of each source of income. Any part of the hotel which is not exclusive to a particular source will be ignored, since the expenses relating to that part will have to be paid out of the income from all sources. This means that in an hotel with a restaurant and kitchen, bar, public rooms, reception, offices, and service areas on the ground floor, and bedrooms on the first and second floors, the allocation would be as follows:

Restaurant: floor area of restaurant, kitchen, and still room.
Bar: floor area of bar and wine cellar.
Rooms: floor area of the whole of the first and second floors.

If the expenses were apportioned to the whole floor area including service areas, and the expense of the service areas thus allocated were then apportioned between the three sources of income, the result would be exactly the same as ignoring the floor area of service areas in the first place. With regard to the service areas on the first and second floors, these should be included with rooms, since they serve no other purpose. In this example the part of the hotel occupied by rooms includes the whole of the two upper floors, in which the restaurant and bar have no interest. On the other hand, a ground-floor lounge, for instance, would serve restaurant, bar, and accommodation.

Example

An hotel has all its bedrooms on the first and second floors, a restaurant, bar, and public rooms on the ground floor.
   Floor areas are as follows:

		sq. m
Ground floor	Restaurant	1,600
	Kitchens	1,200
	Bar and wine cellar	600
	Lounge	900
	Reception, offices, corridors, etc.	800
First floor	Bedrooms	4,400
	Corridors, service areas, etc.	700
Second floor	Bedrooms	4,000
	Corridors, service areas, etc.	500

Wages and expenses for the month of June have been allocated directly to restaurant, bar, or rooms so far as possible, but indirect costs amounting to £3,510 must be apportioned on a floor area basis, with a weighting of 1.5, 1.0, and 1.0 to ground, first, and second floors respectively.
   The relative floor areas are:

		sq. m
Restaurant	$1,600 + 1,200 = 2,800 \times 1.5 =$	4,200
Bar	$600 \times 1.5 =$	900
Accommodation	$4,400 + 700 + 4,000 + 500 = 9,600 \times 1.0 =$	9,600
		14,700

		£
Charge to Restaurant	$4{,}200/14{,}700 \times £3{,}510 =$	1,003
Bar	$900/14{,}700 \times £3{,}510 =$	215
Accommodation	$9{,}600/14{,}700 \times £3{,}510 =$	2,292
		3,510

Exercises

1 The Seaview Hotel has forty bedrooms with a maximum occupancy of 500 bed/nights per week. The hotel is open throughout the year and has an average occupancy rate of 60 per cent.

Meals provided to guests have been costed, and the average food cost is as follows:

Breakfast	£1.20
Lunch	£2.40
Dinner	£3.60

Wages and staff meals amount to £1,105.20 per week for restaurant and kitchen, £658.80 per week for housekeeping, and £306.00 per week general. Overheads amount to £138,060 pa (52 weeks)

You are required to calculate what inclusive terms for full board should be charged per person per week in order to make a net profit equivalent to 15 per cent of takings.

2 A hotel has 100 bedrooms occupying 10,000 sq. metres, each room containing twin beds. The restaurant and kitchen occupy 5,000 sq. metres, the bar 1,000 sq. metres, and general areas 2,000 sq. metres.

The hotel is seasonal, average occupancy for 20 weeks being 90 per cent, and for the remainder of the year 50 per cent (treat the year as 364 days). Direct costs of accommodation amount to £216,475 pa, and general hotel overheads amount to £301,000 pa.

What average charge per person per night for accommodation only should be made to achieve a net profit of 15 per cent of sales?

3 The Moors Hotel has bedrooms giving a full occupany of 400 bed-nights per week, a restaurant, and bar. Average occupancy is 70 per cent.

Direct wages are:	Accommodation	£600 pw
	Restaurant	£400 pw
	Bar	£180 pw
Direct expenses are:	Accommodation	£200 pw
	Restaurant	£150 pw
	Bar	£140 pw

Indirect wages are £600 pw and indirect expenses £52,000 per annum. A net profit of 20 per cent is expected.

Floor areas are: bedrooms 6,000 sq.m, restaurant and kitchen 3,000 sq.m, bar 1,000 sq.m, and service areas 1,000 sq.m.

You are required to work out a reasonable average charge per week per person for accommodation only.

18 Non-profit-making concerns

A works canteen may charge the employees who use it prices which are deliberately less than economic, as a benefit to the employees provided by the company, and if this is so, the calculation of gross profit percentage on selling price will be irrelevant. However, although the canteen may not be required to make a profit, it will still be required to ensure that any loss shall be kept within bounds.

The critical factor is how much subsidy the catering can expect from the company. If it is to be fully subsidised, the costs must be kept within the budgeted subsidy. If a charge for meals is to be made, then the total charges must equal the total of food cost, labour cost, and overheads, less the agreed amount of any subsidy. The total of the estimates of these costs less subsidy is therefore the total amount to be recovered from sales, and if divided by the number of meals expected to be sold, will show the average selling price per meal. When this is compared with the expected average food cost per meal, the percentage supplement to the food cost of each meal will be discovered. This pricing policy of adding a given percentage can be applied to the food cost of each dish, so that a selling price can be calculated – one which will be in the same proportion as the average selling price is to the average food cost.

When a subsidy comes into any calculations, it should be remembered that this should be deducted from the canteen costs, not added to the sales. The subsidy represents that part of the costs which do not have to be paid by the canteen, and the calculations should be dealt with in that way or the results will be misleading.

Question

A factory canteen caters for an average of 100 lunches every working day. It operates 5 days per week for 50 weeks per year. It is estimated that in the coming year food cost will average 40p per meal, labour cost will amount to £135 per week throughout the year, and other costs payable by the canteen will amount to £2,980 in the year.

Calculate the average selling price which will need to be charged if the company subsidises the wages and other costs to the extent of £5,000, and recommend a pricing policy to achieve this result.

Answer

		£
Number of meals	$100 \times 5 \times 50 = 25,000$	
Food cost	$25,000 \times 40p$	10,000
Labour cost	$£135 \times 52$	7,020
Other costs		2,980
		20,000
Less subsidy		5,000
Total sales will need to be		15,000
Average selling price £15,000/25,000		0.60
Average food cost		0.40
Supplement		0.20

Supplement as a percentage of food cost $0.20 \times 100/0.40 = 50\%$

Pricing policy – make the selling price of each dish equal to the food cost of that dish plus a supplement of 50 per cent.

Note that although the canteen is serving meals for only 50 weeks in the year, the canteen staff will still have to be paid for 52 weeks.

Question

A works canteen serves only lunches on 230 days during the year, and is used on average by 125 employees every day that it is open.

In the coming year it is expected that a variety of meals will be served, for which the average food cost is estimated at £0.64 per meal. Canteen staff wages will be £278 per week payable for the full 52 weeks in the year. Canteen overheads are estimated at £6,469 for the year.

The company is willing to subsidise the canteen costs to the extent of £10,000, all remaining costs to be recovered from the prices charged to the employees for meals taken.

(a) Prepare a canteen costs statement showing the estimated total costs of the canteen to be recovered from the employees next year, and the average charge to be made per meal.
(b) Calculate what mark-up percentage must be added to the food cost of each dish to determine the selling price (percentage to the nearest whole number).
(c) Calculate what price should be charged to employees for a dish for which the food cost is £0.48 (selling price to nearest 1p).

Answer

(a)   *Canteen costs statement 19../19..*
No. of meals sold in year 125 × 230   28,750

		£
Total food cost	£0.64 × 28,750	18,400
Staff wages	£278 × 52	14,456
Overheads		6,469
Total costs		39,325
Less subsidy		10,000
Total charge to employees		29,325
Average charge per meal £29,325/28,750		1.02

(b)
Mark-up per meal = £1.02 − £0.64 = £0.38
Mark-up %   = £0.38 × 100/£0.64   59%

(c)
Food cost of dish	0.48
Mark-up 59% of £0.48	0.28
Selling price	0.76

Exercises

1   An industrial canteen caters for an average of 120 lunches per day for 5 days per week, 50 weeks per year. It is estimated that food cost will average 70p per meal, labour cost will be £7,380 per year, and overheads will be £3,120 per year.
    Calculate the average selling price per meal in order for the canteen to break even, and recommend a pricing policy to achieve this result.

2   The Acme Engineering Co Ltd has 200 employees who all take lunch in the works canteen 5 days each week for 50 weeks in the year. The whole company closes down for the other 2 weeks' paid holiday each year.
    Employees are charged 50p per day for lunch, the company subsidising canteen losses. Food cost is £35,500 for the year, canteen wages £9,270, and overheads £5,840.
    Prepare a statement showing the total annual costs of the canteen, the amount recovered from the employees, and the subsidy required from the company.

3   Tempered Steel Ltd operates a works canteen, for which the company is willing to subsidise the costs to the extent of £10,000.
    The canteen serves only lunches from Monday to Friday

inclusive throughout the year, except for 2 weeks' summer holiday and other short holidays totalling an extra week. On average 100 employees use the canteen every day that it is open.

It is estimated that in the coming year 60 per cent of customer orders will be for roasts, 30 per cent for grills, and 10 per cent for snacks.

The cost of canteen staff is £145.00 per week throughout the year, and canteen overheads will be £5,694 for the year. The cost of ingredients is estimated at £1.00 for a roast meal, 80p for a grill, and 40p for a snack.

(a) Prepare a statement showing the estimated total costs of the canteen to be recovered from the employees next year.
(b) Show what percentage supplement on food cost must be used in fixing prices.
(c) Calculate what menu prices will be charged for a roast, a grill, and a snack.

19   Control of food, wines, and takings

Efficient control of food and wine is necessary to avoid loss due to waste, pilfering, or bad buying, and should be carefully enforced from the time the goods enter the premises until they are served to the customer. At that point the care changes into control of takings.

Buying records

It is axiomatic that only goods received should be paid for, only goods ordered should be received, and only goods needed should be ordered, so a checking system which follows all these steps should be enforced. Whether the details are hand-written or computerised, the system should provide for:

1   Ordering should be checked by a responsible member of staff, and a permanent record kept, even if the order itself is given by telephone.
2   When goods are received, the delivery note should immediately be checked with the goods, and later checked with the record of the order. It is useful to have a cross-reference from one to the other in case of later dispute.
3   When the invoice is received, it should be checked with the order or delivery note for quantities, and prices checked for approval by a responsible member of staff. If mistakes are made in pricing, they must be noticed and corrected. If prices have changed, they must be noticed for checking of costings. It is useful for documents to be signed as checked by whoever does the approving.
4   When the statement for payment is received, it should be checked against the invoices before being approved for payment.

Portion control

Portion control is a term which has been widely recognised in the past, but generally misunderstood. It should be used to mean *control* of portion size, so that portions are consistently the same size and not subject to impetuous fluctuation. Without it portions will sometimes be smaller than they should be, and sometimes larger. The differences are likely to cause dissatisfaction among the customers, and havoc with the dish costings. In no other trade would buying and selling take place without the quantity to be sold being specified and strictly controlled, so why should the selling of meals be an exception? The menu prices will have been decided on the basis of dish costings specifying what ingredients will be used per portion, and this needs supervision so that portions do not vary. If the portions specified are too small, it is a different matter, which is nothing to do with portion control, and should be put right forthwith. New costings should then be prepared on the new portion sizes.

The method of achieving portion control is based on being systematic in the preparation and serving of dishes:

1 Recipes should be consistently followed without allowing deviations for 'artistic flair'. If a deviation is good enough to bother with, it should be incorporated in the recipe, included in the dish costing, and always followed thereafter.
2 Suitable equipment should be used, such as scales, measuring jugs, graded scoops and ladles in the kitchen; standard size cups, glasses, and soup bowls in the restaurant.
3 Records such as portion charts must be available to staff to show what sizes are expected and what size scoops, etc., to use.
4 Supervision should be constant, so that a potentially good system does not fail because of new staff or lack of interest.

Food stocks

Whatever the system of recording the stocks of food in hand, it is advisable to make a physical examination of the actual items at regular intervals as a check on the condition of the goods, to make sure that the numbers are as expected (it is not unknown for what was thought to be recorded as 10 dozen to be only 10 single items), and as confirmation of the location where things can be found. It is possible for a whole batch of stock to be mislaid if its absence is not brought to light by a physical check.

If monthly profit figures are prepared, it will be necessary to have stock figures at the end of each month, and the physical check may be made then. If a perpetual inventory is kept, the end of month figures can be taken from this, and the physical check can be done piecemeal instead of all at once, and at a time which is most convenient instead of having to be done at the close of business at the month end.

Once the quantities of stocks in hand have been listed, the values should be priced at cost, which is not always easy to determine. Particularly for items such as tinned goods, which may be bought in quantity at intervals and at different prices, it is sometimes difficult to be sure of the original cost of issues or of stock-in-hand. The particular goods may have been bought at the beginning of the year at £4.87 per dozen, 3 months later at £5.12 per dozen, or later still at £5.24 per dozen, and unless the purchases at one price greatly outnumber the others, it will be difficult to decide which price to use.

In such cases there are two main methods in common use, known as LIFO

(Last In, First Out) and FIFO (First In, First Out). The former assumes that issues will be from the latest purchases and priced accordingly, stocks remaining being priced at the earlier prices. FIFO, on the other hand, assumes that issues are from the earliest purchases, and stocks remaining are priced at the latest prices. Note that this is concerned only with deciding what prices to use in the accounting, and has nothing to do with the good store management principle of always issuing those goods which have been on the shelves longest. The storeman will want to ensure that the first goods to come in are the first goods to go out, but there is a good argument for *pricing* issues at the latest prices, so that costing figures are not prepared at out-of-date prices. There are sound arguments both ways, and in the long run it will make no difference whether the policy adopted is LIFO or FIFO, so long as they are not mixed.

Example

During the quarter ended 31 October 19.. purchases and issues of 822 g canned fruit cocktail were as follows:

	Purchased		*Issued*
August	3 doz @ 68p each =	£24.48	30
September	2½ doz @ 69p each =	£20.70	26
October	2 doz @ 70p each =	£16.80	25
		£61.98	

The value of goods to be accounted for is £61.98, and the total value of goods issued and remaining in stock at the end must add up to this figure. Whichever method is chosen, it must be consistently used without variation.

LIFO method				£	£
August	issues	30 @ 68p			20.40
	stock remaining	6 @ 68p			
September	issues	26 @ 69p			17.94
	stock remaining	4 @ 69p			
		6 @ 68p			
October	issues	24 @ 70p	16.80		
		1 @ 69p	0.69		17.49
	stock remaining	3 @ 69p	2.07		
		6 @ 68p	4.08		6.15
					61.98

FIFO method				£	£
August	issues	30 @ 68p			20.40
	stock remaining	6 @ 68p			
September	issues	6 @ 68p		4.08	
		20 @ 69p		13.80	17.88
	stock remaining	10 @ 69p			

			£	£
October	issues	10 @ 69p	6.90	
		15 @ 70p	10.50	17.40
	stock remaining	9 @ 70p		6.30
				61.98

Other methods of valuing issues of stock include the *average cost method* and the *replacement cost method*. The former depends on finding the new average cost of stock held when each new purchase is made. Issues are valued at this average cost until a new purchase necessitates a new average calculation. The replacement cost method is an extension of LIFO in that issues are valued at the price which would be paid to replace them, whether any goods have already been bought at that price or not. These are not by any means the only methods in use, but whatever method is used, it should be used consistently.

Bar stocks

The gross profit expected from sales of wines and spirits will be lower than from sales of meals, because the costs to be met out of it are not so high. There is no cost of cooking to be covered by the gross profit, so that the usual pricing policy for restaurant sales of wines and spirits is a mark-up of 100 per cent, i.e. doubling the cost, which will give a gross profit of 50 per cent on sales. This is a rule of thumb which is widely followed, but is by no means universal, some establishments taking the view that this is a luxury trade which can be charged for at a higher rate.

The control of bar stocks is an important matter to a catering business, and, if not properly handled, can become a headache. The nature of the commodity is such that any slackness in control presents an intolerable temptation to those who have access to the stock, so that losses may occur, and they will be difficult to detect and prevent. If to this is added a mixing of bar sales or purchases with food sales or purchases, the calculation of profit or loss on both operations will be misleading from the start, so it is important to keep the dealings separate.

Bar stocks have one big advantage from the point of view of control: the bottle is an easily counted unit for which a standard price is charged. This is important because it enables a check to be kept on the comings and goings of stock by valuing all figures of purchases and stock-in-hand at selling price. The actual receipts from sales are already at selling price, so these can be reconciled with the calculated figure of what the sales should be.

Example

Bar stocks control for . . . October 19..

	£
Opening stock at selling price	1,181
Purchases at selling price	2,467
	3,648
Deduct closing stock at selling price	1,063
Calculated sales	2,585
Actual sales	2,604
Surplus (0.7% of calculated sales)	19

In making this calculation allowance must be made for any known breakages, transfers to kitchen, staff allowances, drawings by proprietors, or other reasons for deficiency. In all these cases it is a matter of adjusting the figures for known discrepancies, so that there will be no doubt of something being wrong if the figures do not then reconcile within a reasonable tolerance. It will not be possible to reconcile exactly if mixed drinks are sold because of differences in pricing the proportions of beer and lemonade in a shandy, or the accumulated effect of slight variations in the measures of spirit dispensed by optics. The usual effect of these discrepancies is to produce a surplus, i.e. the actual sales should be greater than the calculated figure. The surplus will vary from one establishment to another, but should be reasonably consistent for the same place from month to month. If there is no surplus, or the surplus is less than usual, investigation should be made into the cause, which may be loss of stock or loss of takings.

Takings

Control of takings entails ensuring that customers are properly charged for all goods and services supplied to them, and that payments by the customers are received in full and properly accounted for.

In the restaurant the method most successfully used is the triplicate checking system, under which a waiter's check book has numbered checks in triplicate, from which one copy goes to the kitchen and one copy goes to the cashier for the preparation of the bill. The numbering ensures that it is always possible to check back between the waiter, the kitchen, and the cashier. Charged bills are sent to the customers' accounts office for entering on the customers' bills. In the control office all the records are checked against each other to ensure that everything has been properly charged.

A similar check system may be used by an hotel for other items which need to be charged, such as room service, laundry, telephone calls, or bar drinks. In each case one copy will be sent to be charged to the customer's account, and another copy or the book of check counterfoils will go to the control office for checking.

Exercises

1 (a) Explain briefly what is meant by the terms LIFO and FIFO.
   (b) From the following information calculate the value of issues in December and stock remaining on 31 December if the LIFO method is used:

1 October	purchases	48	@ £3.60 per doz
October	issues	20	
1 November	purchases	36	@ £4.50 per doz
November	issues	40	
1 December	purchases	36	@ £5.40 per doz
December	issues	30	

2 The figures of a bar for the month of May are as follows:

	Cost £	Selling Price £
Sales		1,114
Purchases	658	1,316
Stock at 1 May	126	252
Stock at 31 May	232	464
Allowances	11	22

Calculate:

(a) The gross profit percentage of sales.
(b) The calculated sales on control at selling price.
(c) The surplus as a percentage of calculated sales.

20 Marginal costing

The effect of some costs being fixed in amount whatever the output is that it is impossible to generalise about the cost per unit of items sold, whether they be meals or hotel bed-nights. The cost per meal or per bed-night can be stated for a given level of output, but this will not be true for a different level.

On the other hand, some costs are variable with output, in that they are directly related to single units of sales. If we calculate the cost of food included in a dish, allowing for an average cost of wastage on a quantity of dishes being apportioned to each dish, this will be the food cost per dish, however many dishes we sell. Some costs are semi-variable in that they will increase or reduce with changes in volume of sales, but not in proportion. Expenses such as renewals of cutlery will be greater if there are many more customers, but possibly no more if there are only a few more customers. What increase there will be in semi-variable expenses if there is a small increase in sales cannot be calculated; it can only be estimated from knowledge of the business.

Once the total increase in semi-variable costs for a number of additional sales has been estimated, this increase can be divided to ascertain the estimated increased cost per sale. If this increase in semi-variable cost per sale is added to the variable cost per sale; the total thus produced is the extra cost of selling one more unit, which is known as the *marginal cost*.

Marginal cost is defined as 'the increase or reduction in total cost, at a given volume of output, resulting from an increase or reduction of one unit of output'. In other words, if we sell one more item, our costs will increase by the marginal cost; if we sell one fewer, our costs will go down by the marginal cost. Note that it is related to a specific volume of sales. For a different level of sales the marginal cost will be different because of the effect of semi-variable costs.

The term marginal costing is used to describe the technique of identifying this extra cost of extra output, and providing guidance on whether the extra business is worth doing. In other industries the technique has relevance to the valuation of work-in-progress, but in hotels and catering there are two main applications – considering whether to accept proposed extra business at a reduced tariff, and whether to open in the off-season.

Extra business at reduced tariff

When looking at the costs of an hotel for a normal year, one may note that the total cost per bed-night works out at (say) £11.50, and, this being the normal business of the hotel, every sale will be expected to pay for this cost and contribute its due proportion of net profit. Once all this normal business has been completed, if the hotel contemplates selling some extra bed-nights, what is the minimum charge which must be made for the extra business to be profitable?

It might be thought that the charge must be more than the cost £11.50 per bed-night, but it should be remembered that this figure includes fixed costs, and there will be no extra fixed costs to be met out of the extra takings. If a tour operator proposes a block booking out of season at a reduced tariff of £11.00 per bed-night, at first sight it is not immediately apparent whether the extra business will be profitable. Provided the proposal does not interfere with normal business, what matters is whether the proposed selling price is more or less than the marginal cost. If the selling price is greater than the marginal cost, then more profit will be made by accepting the proposal than by refusing it. The question of whether the extra business will help in retaining staff is a different matter, which may be vital in reaching a decision, but is separate from this question of profitability.

Question

An hotel sells on average 20,000 bed-nights a year, and achieves the following results

	Per year £	Per bed-night £
Sales	400,000	20.00
Food cost	108,000	5.40
Fixed costs	65,000	3.25
Variable expenses	42,000	2.10
Semi-variable expenses	135,000	6.75
	350,000	17.50
Net profit	50,000	2.50

A tour operator proposes to bring coach parties out of season totalling 400 extra bed-nights at a charge inclusive of food of £12.00 per person per night. It is estimated that this would cause an increase of £980 in semi-variable expenses. As the proposed charge is not only less than the normal charge of £20.00, but less than the total cost per bed-night of £17.50, should the proposal be rejected?

Answer

The marginal cost is as follows:

	£
Food cost	5.40
Variable expenses	2.10
Semi-variable expenses (£980/400)	2.45
	9.95

Food cost and variable expenses are both variable costs, which means that every extra sale incurs the same cost as previous sales. The semi-variable expenses incurred by the extra sales are £980 for 400 extra sales, or £2.45 per sale. The amount of semi-variable expenses incurred by the previous sales relates only to the previous sales, the extra cost of the extra business being what matters.

Since the marginal cost is less than the proposed charge for the extra business, there will be a positive *contribution* to profit of £2.05 per bed-night (£12.00 − £9.95), so from the financial point of view the proposal should be accepted. The extra business will result in making £820 extra profit (400 extra bed-nights × £2.05 contribution per bed-night), which is a quicker and more informative calculation than estimating the total amounts.

Annual results with extra business

	£
Sales £400,000 + £4,800 (400 × £12.00)	404,800
Food cost £108,000 + £2,160 (400 × £5.40)	110,160
Fixed expenses (unchanged)	65,000
Variable expenses £42,000 + £840 (400 × £2.10)	42,840
Semi-variable expenses £135,000 + £980	135,980
	353,980
Net profit £50,000 + £820	50,820

Off-season opening

In considering the advisability of opening during what would otherwise be a close season, you will need to take many factors into account, in addition to the purely financial result, such as the difficulty of re-engaging staff after closing down, the benefit of keeping the premises heated during the winter, and uninterrupted marketing. Whether the project is financially worthwhile will be shown very simply by marginal costing. The extra unit of output will be the off-season period of time, and the estimated sales for the period should be compared with the marginal cost to find the contribution made.

Question

The financial results of a restaurant for last year were as follows:

	Season £	Off-season £	Year £
Sales	66,000	24,000	90,000
Variable costs	39,600	14,400	54,000
Semi-variable costs	9,000	6,000	15,000
Fixed costs	4,500	4,500	9,000
	53,100	24,900	78,000
Net profit (loss)	12,900	(900)	12,000

Since a loss was made in the off-season, would it have been better to close during that period?

Answer

In a word, no! The fixed expenses allocated to the off-season would still have to be met out of the takings of the season if the restaurant closed. It is assumed that costs have been analysed so that only inescapable costs have been described as fixed costs, and that semi-variable costs are those relating exclusively to business done in the relevant period.

The contribution of the off-season is:

	£
Sales	24,000
Marginal cost (£14,400 + £6,000)	20,400
Contribution	3,600

This illustrates the reason for the contribution being referred to as a contribution to fixed costs and profit. In this case the off-season is making a positive contribution of £3,600 towards the inescapable costs of £4,500, leaving £900 of those costs not covered. But this is better than not covering any of those costs during the off-season, in which case the net profit for the year would be £3,600 less:

Annual profit if closed during off-season

	£
Sales (season only)	66,000
Variable costs	39,600
Semi-variable costs	9,000
Fixed costs (whole year's rent, rates, etc.)	9,000
	57,600
Net profit	8,400

Exercises

1 The following figures relate to a seasonal restaurant:

	April–September £	October–March £
Sales	126,000	42,000
Cost of sales	50,400	16,800
Wages and salaries	30,000	24,000
Light and heat	1,500	1,800
Cleaning, etc.	450	450
Other variable expenses	1,500	1,500
Fixed expenses £12,900 pa		

On the basis of the above figures, would it be financially better to open for the full year or only from April to September?

2 The Headland Hotel's occupancy averages 10,000 bed-nights per year, and sales and costs for next year have been estimated as follows:

	£
Sales	300,000
Food cost	80,000
Labour cost	66,000
Fixed expenses	48,000
Variable expenses	27,000
Semi-variable expenses	44,000

It is now proposed that special terms should be offered to guests booking for a week on full-board tariff in October and November next year. Arising out of this, it is expected that an additional 490 bed-nights would be sold at £20.00 per person per night. The extra business would result in additional wages amounting to £1,274, and additional semi-variable expenses amounting to £1,666.

You are required to:

(a) Calculate the marginal cost of the additional business.
(b) Show, by reference to the contribution, what additional profit will be made from the 490 extra bed-nights.
(c) State what is the lowest charge per week which could be made for the extra business without operating at a loss.

3 During a normal year a restaurant sells 120,000 covers, and produces the following results:

	£
Sales	720,000
Food cost	288,000
Gross profit	432,000
Fixed labour cost and overheads	168,000
Variable costs	84,000
Semi-variable costs	105,000
	357,000
Net profit	75,000

Of the semi-variable costs, £85,000 is a basic minimum needed for up to 80,000 covers, and the amount increases by £500 for every additional 1,000 covers.

It is proposed to use an annexe as a popular self-service restaurant, selling the same dishes at a 15 per cent price reduction. Additional fixed costs of £33,000 pa would be incurred, but it is estimated that an additional 50,000 covers would be sold.

If the estimates are correct, should the scheme be adopted? How many covers would the new department have to sell in order to break even?

4 As banqueting manager of a large hotel, you are asked to consider three alternative functions proposed for the same evening, and to decide which one should be accepted.

Your assistant has calculated the profit figures as follows:

	Function A	Function B	Function C
Number of covers	70	90	40
	£	£	£
Selling price per cover	15.00	15.00	15.00
Costs per cover:			
Food	8.70	9.30	8.25
Extra staff	0.90	0.75	1.35
Additional expenses	0.60	0.90	1.05
Fixed expenses	0.75	0.75	0.75
	10.95	11.70	11.40
Net profit per cover	4.05	3.30	3.60

The fixed expenses have been calculated at £0.75 per cover on the basis of total annual fixed expenses of £75,000 divided by the average number of 100,000 covers served in a year.

You are required to:

(a) Prepare a statement showing the contribution from each function.
(b) State which function should be accepted.
(c) Comment on the method used by your assistant in calculating the comparative profitability.

21   Graphic presentation

Financial information can often be more readily appreciated if it is presented in the form of suitable illustrations instead of columns of figures. A pie chart is useful to illustrate how a total is divided up, a bar chart is ideal for comparisons, and a contribution chart is a graph which shows at a glance what profitability may be expected at any point over a range of sales.

Whatever kind of chart is used, it should be clearly headed to show what kind of information is being presented, and each factor shown should be identified. The point about graphic representation is that it should be readily understood, and this point is lost if the chart needs careful study by an expert to see what it is all about.

Pie chart

This is a simple circle supposed to be a pie representing a total which is to be divided between component parts. In this sense it is commonly used to illustrate the elements of sales.

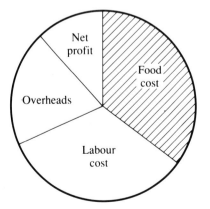

Figure 21.1   *Where the income goes*

In Figure 21.1 food cost is 40 per cent of sales, and is shaded. The unshaded part of the circle is gross profit (60 per cent), which is further divided into labour cost (28 per cent), overheads (20 per cent), and net profit (12 per cent).

Other popular uses for a pie chart are to show the sales mix of a business, or the parts relating to divisions in group figures.

Bar chart

This is an illustration of blocks (or bars) of various heights standing side by side for comparison. Each block may represent the sales for a different month, or any other matter where the visual comparison of size is easier to assimilate than the raw data. See Figure 21.2.

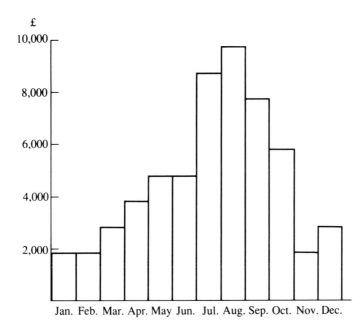

Figure 21.2 *Monthly sales*

Fixed and variable costs

If all costs varied in proportion to sales, then every sale would be profitable, e.g.

	£
1 sale @ £3.00	3.00
Less cost per unit £2.60	2.60
Net profit	0.40

3,000

1,000 sales @ £3.00	3,000
Less cost per unit £2.60	2,600
Net profit (1,000 × £0.40)	400

But some costs are fixed in amount, and need to be paid out of a number of sales (e.g. rent £1,000). If the only costs were fixed, the number of sales required to cover the fixed costs would be fixed costs divided by the selling price per unit, e.g. if SP is £4.00 each and total costs (all fixed) are £1,000, then it is necessary to sell 250 items in order to break even.

Break-even chart

When some costs are variable and some fixed, the variable costs may be regarded as being over and above the fixed costs, which have to be paid anyway, whether there are any sales or not. This is the basis used for a break-even chart, which is a graph with the *x* axis or baseline representing a range of sales, and the *y* axis representing the money value of income and costs plotted on the chart. The level of sales may be expressed in money terms or in numbers of sales. If it is expressed in numbers, e.g. numbers of meals sold, the income may be plotted as the money value of sales, but if sales are shown on the *x* axis, then instead of plotting sales and total costs, it is usual to reduce the size of the graph by plotting gross profit and costs other than food cost.

If the plots of income (sales or gross profit) are connected by lines, and similarly the plots of costs, the difference between the two lines is net profit, where the income line is higher than costs, or net loss, where the costs line is higher than the income. Break-even point is that level of sales where one line crossed the other, i.e. where costs are equal to income. See Figure 21.3.

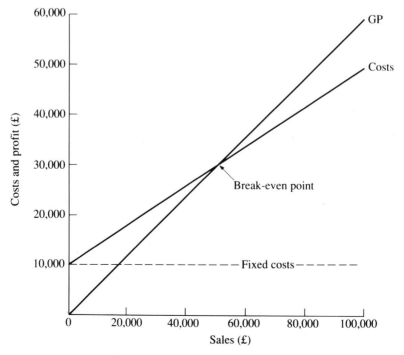

Figure 21.3   *Break-even chart*

The fixed costs are the same amount whatever the level of sales, and are therefore represented by a horizontal line across the chart. The variable costs are over and above the fixed costs, and are shown that way on the chart, so the rising costs line represents the total amount of fixed plus variable costs for any level of sales within the range shown. Food cost is not included in this because it has already been deducted from the gross profit.

Question

A new restaurant is being planned, and the following estimates are made for the first year of operation:

1   Maximum occupancy will be 480 covers per week.
2   The average price charged for a meal will be £6.00.
3   Fixed expenses in the first year will be £15,600.
4   Dish costings are calculated to give a gross profit of 65 per cent of sales.
5   Labour cost is expected to be 25 per cent of sales.
6   Variable expenses are estimated at 15 per cent of sales.

(a) Show the calculation of how many meals would have to be sold each week in order to break even.
(b) Express break-even point as an occupancy percentage.
(c) Prepare a break-even chart showing the profitability resulting from numbers of meals sold, ranging from 0 to 480 per week, indicating the break-even point and the range of profitability.

Answer

(a) Fixed expenses £15,600 pa = £300 per week.
      Sales = food cost + labour cost + overheads + net profit
      Sales at BEP = food 35% + labour 25% + var. exs 15% + fixed exs £300 + nil
      Sales at BEP = 75% of sales + £300: so £300 = 25% of sales at BEP
                = £300 × 100/25 = £1,200
      BEP in meals sold is £1,200 /£6 = 200 meals per week
(b) Occupancy at BEP is 200 × 100/480 = 41.7%

(c)

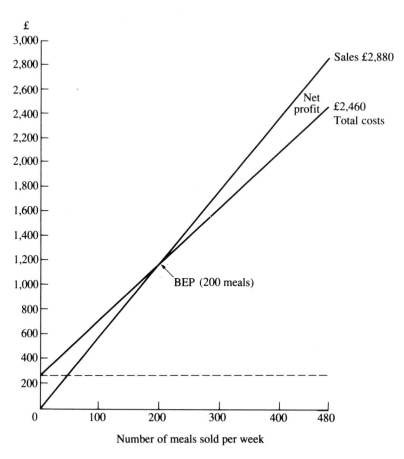

Figure 21.4   *Break-even chart*

Contribution chart

Another way of looking at the question of fixed and variable costs is to say that every sale will have to pay for its variable cost, and what is left (contribution) will go towards the fixed cost and profit, e.g.

	£
1 sale @ £5.00	5.00
Less variable cost per unit	4.00
Contribution	1.00
Fixed costs	10,000.00
Net loss	9,999.00

	£
10,000 sales @ £5.00	50,000
Less variable cost @ £4.00 each	40,000
Contribution (10,000 × £1)	10,000
Fixed costs	10,000
	Break even
20,000 sales @ £5.00	100,000
Less variable cost @ £4.00 each	80,000
Contribution (20,000 × £1)	20,000
Fixed costs	10,000
Net profit	10,000

The contribution chart is a graph showing the contribution to fixed costs and profit to be expected over a range of business done. Again the range can be measured in sales money or numbers of items sold. It is a development of the break-even chart, and answers the criticism that the title 'break-even chart' puts too much emphasis on only one item of information shown by the graph – the level of sales at which the business would break even. In fact it is likely to be of more interest to see what profit can be expected at other levels of sales, and for a business regularly making profits, the contribution chart may start at such a high level of sales that break-even point does not show on it.

The baseline represents a net profit of nil, so any result above the line is a net profit, and anything below the line is a net loss. Where the contribution crosses the baseline is of course break-even point, as at that level of sales there is no profit or loss. At nil sales the contribution is a minus figure equal to the fixed costs, and for every sale thereafter there will be a contribution to the fixed costs until they have been fully covered. From there on every extra sale makes a contribution to net profit. See Figure 21.5.

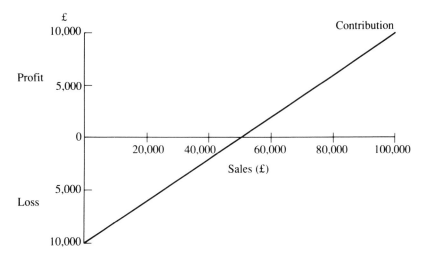

Figure 21.5   *Contribution chart*

For an established business this chart could very well be drawn with the *x* axis starting at £60,000 sales, if the range of possible business is not likely to fall below that, so that the chart would be more detailed about the likely results instead of showing so much information about the unlikely event of sales being nil. See Figure 21.6.

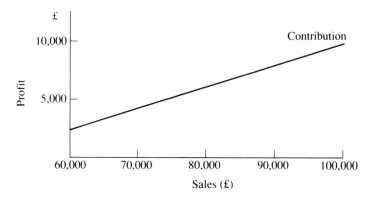

Figure 21.6   *Contribution chart*

Question

Prepare a contribution chart for a restaurant covering a range of business from 10,000 to 20,000 covers sold. Average selling price is £8.00 per cover, and the menu prices are calculated on the basis of a mark-up of 150 per cent on food cost. Labour cost averages 20 per cent of sales, fixed expenses amount to £15,000 pa, and variable expenses are 5 per cent of sales.

Answer

Mark-up is 150 per cent of food cost, so food cost is 100/250 × 100% of sales
Variable cost is food 40% + labour 20% + var. exs 5% = 65% of sales
Contribution is £8.00 − £5.20 (65% of £8) = £2.80 per meal

See also Figure 21.7.

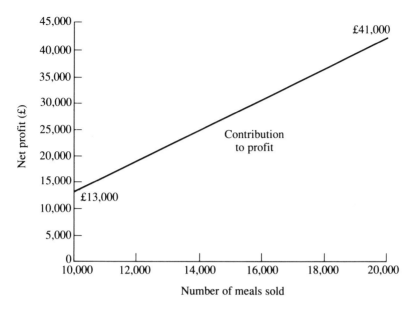

Figure 21.7   *Contribution chart*

In preparing any graph it is worth spending some time to get your scale right, bearing in mind the information you have to show and the graph paper you are going to use. Do not pick a scale with steps of 3 units, 300, or 3,000. Plotting becomes so difficult as to make mistakes almost inevitable. Choose units of 2 or 5, which can be plotted easily on graph paper, even if it means not using all the paper available.

Exercises

1   Prepare a break-even chart for a restaurant covering a range of business from 0 to 30,000 covers sold.

Average selling price is £7.50 per cover, and the restaurant prices its menus on the basis of a mark-up of 150 per cent on food cost. Labour cost averages 20 per cent of sales, fixed expenses amount to £45,000 pa, and variable expenses are 4 per cent of sales. Calculate break-even point and indicate where it occurs on your graph.

2   A new restaurant is being opened, and maximum occupancy is expected to be 1,200 covers per week.

Costs for the first year of operation are estimated at £20,800 fixed expenses, variable expenses will be 12 per cent of sales, and labour cost will be 28 per cent of sales. The average selling price of a meal is expected to be £10.00, and dish costings will be calculated to give a gross profit of 60% of sales.

You are required to:

(a) Prepare a break-even chart showing the profitability resulting from numbers of meals sold from 100 to 1,200 per week, indicating the break-even point and range of profitability.

(b) Show the calculation of break-even point in numbers of meals per week.

(c) Express break-even point as an occupancy percentage.

3 A new restaurant is being planned, and the following estimates are made for the first year of operation:

1   The average price charged for a meal will be £8.00.
2   Maximum occupancy will be 480 covers per week.
3   Fixed expenses will be £13,520 pa.
4   Gross profit will be 60 per cent of sales.
5   Labour cost including casual staff will be 25 per cent of sales.
6   Variable expenses will amount to 15 per cent of sales.

(a) You are required to calculate how many meals would have to be sold in order to break even, and show your calculation.

(b) Prepare a contribution chart for the range from 0 to 480 covers per week.

22 *Budgetary control*

The term budgetary control is used to mean control of costs by means of budgets, which are accounting statements based on carefully estimated forecasts of future financial transactions. The budget itself enables future results to be foreseen so that plans can be made accordingly. It also provides a yardstick for comparison with actual results, and a target to aim for.

Budgets may be prepared for any financial matters. They may be revenue statements, including sales budgets, expense budgets, or profit budgets; or capital statements, such as cash budgets, capital expenditure budgets, or projected balance sheets.

Budget committee

The budget statement may be prepared by an individual, but it is not to be expected that any one person could or should attempt alone to make the forecasts from which the statement is put together. The budget should represent the best information obtainable about the probable results in the coming year, and at the same time provide a target which everyone should strive to achieve during the year. For both these reasons the figures in the budget should be provided and agreed by a committee of all those who have responsiblity for running the business, and for seeing that targets are reached. This *budget committee* will make forecasts which must be seen to be realistically achievable, and the figures can then be tabulated in a budget statement.

Operating or profit budgets

A profit budget will usually be prepared for the coming year, divided into convenient shorter accounting periods, so that the accuracy of the budget can be checked at the end of each accounting period. Thus the year may be divided into 12 calendar months, 12 accounting periods of 4 or 5 weeks (two 4-week periods followed by one 5-week period throughout the year), or 13 accounting periods of 4 weeks each. The essence of budgetary control is that actual results shall be compared with the budget figures promptly at the end of each period. At this point the budget may be left unaltered and the actual results noted separately (*fixed budgets*), or the budget may be amended to actual figures up to date so that the budget for the year is constantly made more accurate (*flexible budgets*). The layout of an operating budget statement will take the form of a vertical profit and loss account set out in columns to show the figures for each accounting period and the total for the year.

Operating budget 19../19..

	May	June	July	Aug.	Apr.	Year
Sales	7,500	10,400	14,400	15,500	6,200	105,000
Gross profit	4,500	6,250	8,650	9,300	3,700	63,000
Labour cost	2,250	3,100	4,300	4,650	1,850	31,500
Fixed expenses	800	800	800	800	800	9,600
Variable expenses	750	1,050	1,450	1,550	600	10,500
	3,800	4,950	6,550	7,000	3,250	51,600
Net profit	700	1,300	2,100	2,300	550	11,400

This is evidently a seasonal business with a financial year running from May to April. Sales for the year have been estimated, and the gross profit calculated at the expected percentage of sales, in this example approximately 60 per cent. Labour cost has been estimated at approximately 30 per cent of sales, and variable expenses at approximately 10 per cent. The approximations are to acknowledge the fact that these are estimates and not known results. Too-precise figures can be misleading in this respect, and serve no useful purpose when the actual results will probably be different anyway. For examination work of course the instructions of the examiner must be followed. In practice most expenses are semi-variable, which causes the budget committee more trouble in forecasting, so examiners are forced to treat them as strictly variable or give the amounts in the question.

Question

Budgeted profit figures for a restaurant are required for the year ended 28 February, and for each quarter during the year.

Sales last year amounted to £84,897, and for next year are expected to increase by 10 per cent (estimate total for year to nearest £100). Sales in the quarter ended 31 August are expected to be £46,200, and the sales in the quarter ended February £7,600. Sales in the other two quarters are expected to be equal.

Gross profit is expected to be 60 per cent of sales (to the nearest £10). Wages are estimated at 30 per cent of sales. Fixed expenses amount to £3,800 per annum.

Semi-variable expenses are estimated at £3,320 for the quarter to May, £5,030 for the quarter to August, £3,560 for the quarter to November, and £3,070 for the quarter to February.

Answer

Profit budget 19../19..

	May	Aug.	Nov.	Feb.	Year
Sales	19,800	46,200	19,800	7,600	93,400
Gross profit	11,880	27,720	11,880	4,560	56,040
Wages	5,940	13,860	5,940	2,280	28,020
Fixed expenses	950	950	950	950	3,800
Semi-variable expenses	3,320	5,030	3,560	3,070	14,980
	10,210	19,840	10,450	6,300	46,800
Budgeted net profit	1,670	7,880	1,430	(1,740) Loss	9,240

Cash budgets

A cash budget statement may look very similar to the profit budget, and will use much of the same information; but the emphasis is on the balance of cash available throughout the year, instead of the profit being made. The estimates entered for each month will be the amounts expected to be received or paid in that month, and the balances carried forward from month to month. Capital items which were ignored in estimating profit will be included if there is any movement of cash. Income and expenses other than depreciation will appear in both budgets, but in different months if credit is taken. Period payments, such as insurance premiums, will be shown when they are paid instead of being apportioned over the period for which they are paid. As the balance is carried forward from one month to the next, the balance at the end of the last month will be the balance at the end of the year, and there is no need of a total column. In effect the cash budget becomes a summary of what is expected to appear in the cash book month by month over the coming year.

Question

From the following forecasts prepare a cash budget for the months of June, July, and August 19..

	£
1 June 19.. bank balance	19,600
Sales for May	28,400
Sales for June	31,200
Sales for July	40,800
Sales for August	49,500
Investment income due 30 June 19.., receivable July	1,500
Expenses and wages for May	8,100
Expenses and wages for June	8,700
Expenses and wages for July	10,100
Expenses and wages for August	10,900

	£
Purchases for May	11,200
Purchases for June	12,500
Purchases for July	14,300
Purchases for August	19,800
Rent payable 30 June 19..	4,200
Dividend on share capital payable 1 July 19..	12,000

Allow for 20 per cent of sales being on 1 month's credit, the rest being cash sales. Expenses and wages will be paid in cash, and purchases will all be on 1 month's credit.

Answer

Cash budget 19..

	June £	July £	Aug. £
Receipts			
Cash sales	24,960	32,640	39,600
Credit sales	5,680	6,240	8,160
Investment income		1,500	
	30,640	40,380	47,760
Payments			
Purchases	11,200	12,500	14,300
Rent	4,200		
Expenses	8,700	10,100	10,900
Dividend		12,000	
	24,100	34,600	25,200
Surplus in month	6,540	5,780	22,560
Balance from last month	19,600	26,140	31,920
Balance at end of month	26,140	31,920	54,480

The amount of the expenses and wages for May is ignored in this statement because it would already have appeared in the budget for May.

An alternative layout for a cash budget is to include the cash balance from last month in the cash receipts at the top of the statement, instead of adjusting the balance at the foot of each month. This alternative has the disadvantage of not showing whether the transactions of each month will result in a surplus or deficit, and also as a practical matter it is not so easy to alter the running balances when the budget is revised in the course of preparation.

Alternative layout

	June £	July £	Aug. £
Receipts			
Balance brought forward	19,600	26,140	31,920
Cash sales	24,960	32,640	39,600
Credit sales	5,680	6,240	8,160
Investment income		1,500	
	50,240	66,520	79,680
Payments			
Purchases	11,200	12,500	14,300
Rent	4,200		
Expenses	8,700	10,100	10,900
Dividend		12,000	
	24,100	34,600	25,200
Balance carried forward	26,140	31,920	54,480

Since the estimates used for preparing the cash budget must be the same as those used for preparing the profit budget, the one can be prepared from the other if the following adjustments are made:

1 Allow for credit for payments and receipts.
2 Eliminate depreciation from the figures used in the profit budget.
3 Allow for capital receipts and payments.
4 Enter payments for period expenses when actually made.
5 If stocks have varied, allow for the difference between cost of goods sold and cost of goods purchased.

Question

A restaurant is preparing budgets for the coming financial year, divided into 12 calendar months. The operating budget includes the following:

	May	June	July	Aug.	Sept.
Sales	8,000	10,000	12,000	14,000	12,000
Gross profit	4,800	6,000	7,200	8,400	7,200
Wages	1,900	2,400	2,800	3,300	3,000
Rates	100	100	100	100	100
Insurance	10	10	10	10	10
Depreciation	185	185	185	185	185
Other expenses	1,805	2,055	2,315	2,555	2,305
	4,000	4,750	5,410	6,150	5,600
Net profit	800	1,250	1,790	2,250	1,600

Three-quarters of sales are cash sales, the remainder being on 1 month's credit. Purchases are all on 1 month's credit. Stocks are negligible.

It is forecast that the balance of cash on 1 June will be £3,400. It is expected that new equipment costing £2,000 will be purchased in July, payable after 1 month, and that old equipment will be sold in July for £200 cash.

Rates are payable in two half-yearly instalments on 1 April and 1 October. Insurance is payable annually on 1 August. Wages and other expenses are payable in the month in which they are incurred.

You are required to prepare a cash budget for June, July, and August.

Answer

Cash Budget 19..

	June £	July £	Aug. £
Receipts			
Sales – cash	7,500	9,000	10,500
– credit	2,000	2,500	3,000
Sales of equipment		200	
	9,500	11,700	13,500
Payments			
Purchases	3,200	4,000	4,800
Wages	2,400	2,800	3,300
Insurance			120
Other expenses	2,055	2,315	2,555
New equipment			2,000
	7,655	9,115	12,775
Increase (reduction) in cash	1,845	2,585	725
Balance brought forward	3,400	5,245	7,830
Balance carried forward	5,245	7,830	8,555

It will be noted that although there is no mention of purchases in the operating budget, the amount must be the difference between the sales figures and the gross profit figure each month, and it will be paid in the following month.

Exercises

1   From the following information prepare a revenue budget for the year ended 28 February and for each quarter (calculate all amounts to the nearest £10).

   Sales are estimated at £12,200 for the quarter to May, £23,800 for the quarter to August, £18,600 for the quarter to November, and £9,900 for the quarter to February. Gross profit is estimated at 60 per cent of sales.

Wages and salaries for each quarter will amount to £3,100 for permanent staff, and 12 per cent of turnover over £10,000 for temporary staff. Fixed expenses amount to £9,320 pa. Variable expenses are estimated at 8 per cent of sales.

2   Prepare a profit budget statement for each of the months June, July, and August, and the total for the quarter, using the following information and calculating all amounts to the nearest £10. Show on your statement the net profit percentages for each month and the quarter.

(a) Sales last year were June £4,600 (50 per cent occupancy), July £6,440 (70 per cent occupancy), and August £7,360 (80 per cent occupancy).

(b) As a result of increased advertising it is hoped to increase occupancy to 55 per cent, 75 per cent, and 85 per cent respectively, and it is planned to increase all selling prices by 10 per cent in order to cover the rise in food costs.

(c) Gross profit is expected to be 65 per cent of sales.

(d) Labour costs will be £810 per month for permanent staff, and a further 15 per cent of sales for temporary staff.

(e) Rates will be payable in two equal instalments of £2,100 each in April and October.

(f) Insurance of £720 is payable on the 1 June for 1 year in advance.

(g) Other expenses will be £860 in June, £1,410 in July, and £1,540 in August.

(h) Depreciation for the year is £1,800.

3   The Thames Restaurant prepares budgets each year divided into 12 calendar months, and you are required to show the cash budget for June, July, and August, using the following information:

		£
(a) Sales for May		11,500
	June	13,200
	July	15,700
	August	18,200
	September	17,300

(b) Gross profit is expected to be 60 per cent of sales.

(c) Stocks of food are not expected to vary in amount.

(d) Expenses are forecast for profit purposes as follows:

| | May | June | July | Aug. | Sept. |
	£	£	£	£	£
Wages	2,600	3,400	3,900	4,500	4,100
Rates	240	240	240	240	240
Insurance	30	30	30	30	30
Depreciation	300	300	300	300	300
Other expenses	2,250	3,100	3,600	4,200	3,800

(e) Sales are 50 per cent for cash, 50 per cent on 1 month's credit.

(f) Purchases are all on 1 month's credit.

(g) Wages and other expenses are payable in the month in which they are incurred.

(h) Rates are payable in two half-yearly instalments in April and October.

(i) Insurance is payable annually in July.

(j) It is expected that the balance of cash at bank on 1 June will be £2,900, and new equipment costing £1,500 will be purchased and paid for in August.

23 *Variance analysis*

Standard costing is the practice of estimating standard amounts for all costs, and preparing costing statements from the standard costs instead of from the actual costs. Control is exercised by analysing the differences between these figures and the actual results, and expressing each difference as a *favourable variance* or *adverse variance*, depending on whether the effect of it is to be more profitable or less profitable than expected. The process is known as *variance analysis*, and can be very useful in identifying and allocating responsibility for differences in profit.

The variances in profit will be due to differences from budget in sales, ingredient cost, labour cost, or overheads. In the case of sales, the variance may relate to the unit price, to the volume (number of units), or to the mix if there is more than one kind of sale. With regard to ingredient cost, the variance will be due to changes in the price per unit, or the usage (quantity of ingredients used per meal). The examples given here will relate to sales and food cost variances, but the same principles apply to labour cost and overheads, with some slight changes in the terms used to make them more appropriate. For food we would refer to ingredient price variance, but for wages to wage rate variance instead of wage price variance. Similarly the term efficiency is used instead of usage.

Where only one commodity is being sold, any increase or reduction in total sales can be attributed to one of two causes:

1 A difference in the selling price of each item sold.
2 A difference in the number of items sold.

The variance arising from the first is called a sales margin price variance, and will allow for the change in average selling price for all meals actually sold at the different price. The second is called a sales margin volume variance, and this will automatically create an extra need of ingredients for extra meals, or fewer ingredients for fewer meals, so that the variance will take into account the different number of meals and the standard gross profit on each meal.

An increase or reduction in the total cost of ingredients used may be due to any of three causes:

1 A change in the number of units sold.
2 A change in the buying price of food.
3 A change in the quantity of food used in each meal.

The first is part of the sales margin volume variance already dealt with, the second is an ingredient price variance, and the third is an ingredient usage variance. All these variances are described as favourable or adverse according to their effect on profit.

Example 1

If the actual selling price is different from the standard, but no other changes have taken place, the gross profit will be different by the sales price variance, which is the difference in selling price for all the meals actually sold.

	Budget		*Actual*	
		£		£
Sales	1,000 × £5.00	5,000	1,000 × £4.90	4,900
Food cost	250 kg @ £8.00 kg	2,000	250 kg @ £8.00 kg	2,000
Gross profit		3,000		2,900

Sales margin price
Variance = Difference in SP per meal × actual number of meals.
     = £0.10 reduction (adverse variance) × 1,000
     = £100.00 (adverse)

Notice the step in the reasoning which picks out the relevant change in the selling price of £0.10 and labels it a reduction and therefore *adverse*. This is very helpful in ensuring that your variance is identified correctly, particularly with the more complicated examples.

Example 2

If 200 more meals are sold than expected, the difference in sales will be 200 × selling price per meal, but the profit will not increase by this amount because more meals will mean more food cost. The variance in the profit will be 200 × standard gross profit per meal, which allows for the extra food used to produce the extra meals, assuming that the standard quantity of food is used in each meal. Any further difference in the cost of food actually used will be due to a change in the price paid for food, or a change in the quantity used in each meal, and will show as an ingredient price variance or an ingredient usage variance.

	Budget		*Actual*	
		£		£
Sales	1,000 × £5.00	5,000	1,200 × £5.00	6,000
Food cost	250 kg @ £8.00 kg	2,000	300 kg @ £8.00 kg	2,400
Gross profit (£3.00 per meal)		3,000		3,600

It will be seen that the quantity of food used per meal is 250 g in both standard and actual figures, the increased actual total quantity being due to the extra sales volume. The only variation in gross profit is due to the volume of sales.

Sales margin volume

> Variance = Difference in number of meals × standard GP per meal.
> = 200 more (favourable) × £3.00
> = £600.00 (favourable)

Example 3

Similarly with changes in the cost of food, the variation in gross profit may be due to a change in ingredient price per kg or to a change in the quantity used per meal.

	Budget	£	*Actual*	£
Sales	1,000 × £5.00	5,000	1,000 × £5.00	5,000
Food cost	250 kg @ £8.00 kg	2,000	300 kg @ £8.10 kg	2,430
Gross profit (£3.00 per meal)		3,000		2,570

The gross profit is less only because of a change in food cost, but this itself is due to both an increase in the cost per kg of food and also to using more food in each meal.

Ingredient price variance = Difference in price × actual usage.
> = £0.10 more (adverse) × 300 kg
> = £30.00 (adv.)

Ingredient usage variance = Difference in quantity used per meal × actual number of meals × standard price per kg.
> = 0.05 kg more (adv.) × 1,000 × £8.00 per kg
> = £400.00 (adv.)

Total change in gross profit £430.00 (adv.)

It is possible for all these factors, comprising all four variances, to change. Remember to pick out the price variances first, before volume or usage. Price variances are change in price multiplied by *actual*. Volume and usage are change in numbers multiplied by *standard*.

Example 4

	Budget	£	*Actual*	£
Sales	1,000 × £5.00	5,000	1,100 × £4.90	5,390
Food cost	250 kg @ £8.00 kg	2,000	330 kg @ £8.10 kg	2,673
Gross profit (£3.00 per meal)		3,000		2,717

In this example the extra usage of ingredients, 80 kg, is partly due to increased volume of sales, and partly due to increased usage on each meal, which was the difference between the standard 0.25 kg and the actual 0.3 kg per meal:

Extra ingredients caused by sales volume 100 meals × 0.25 kg		= 25 kg
Extra ingredients caused by ingredient usage 1,100 meals × 0.05 kg		= 55 kg
		80 kg

		£
Sales price variance	£0.10 × 1,100	(110) (adv.)
Sales volume variance	100 × £3.00	300 (fav.)
Ingredient price variance	£0.10 × (1,100 × 0.3 kg = 330 kg)	(33) (adv.)
Ingredient usage variance	0.05 kg × 1,100 meals × £8.00 kg	(440) (adv.)
Net reduction in profit		(283)

The standard food cost is the standard quantity multiplied by the standard purchase price, i.e. £750, but in calculating the usage variance what matters is the standard quantity per meal for the number of meals actually sold. So the usage variance is the difference between the actual and standard usage per meal (actual 0.30 kg − standard 0.25 kg = 0.05 kg) × the number of meals actually sold, at the standard price per kg.

An alternative way of calculating the standard usage is by taking proportions of total quantities, and this is very useful if the quantities per meal are not exact amounts:

Total quantity for standard 1,000 meals	250 kg
Standard quantity for 1,100 meals 1,100/1,000 × 250 kg	275 kg
Actual quantity for 1,100 meals	330 kg
Usage Variance 330 kg − 275 kg = 55 kg @ standard price £8.00	£440 (adv.)

For examination purposes, an examiner may adopt the rather unrealistic device of presenting the information the wrong way round as a test of students' understanding.

Question

The following is a reconciliation of the budgeted and actual gross profit for a catering company:

		£
Budget gross profit 3,000 meals @ £2.67		8,010
Add sales price variance		
Actual	£4.80	
Standard	£4.50	
4,000 meals @	£0.30	1,200
Add sales volume variance		
Actual	4,000 meals	
Standard	3,000 meals	
	1,000 meals @ £2.67	2,670
		11,880

		£
Less ingredient price variance		
Actual	£9.48 per kg	
Standard	£9.15 per kg	
1,000 kg @	£0.33 per kg	330
		11,550
Less ingredient usage variance		
Actual usage at actual volume	1,000 kg	
Standard usage at actual volume	800 kg	
	200 kg @ £9.15	1,830
Actual gross profit 4,000 meals @ 2.43		9,720

You are required to prepare (a) the budget trading account and (b) the actual trading account.

Answer

(a) *Budget trading account*

		£
Sales	3,000 meals @ £4.50 per meal	13,500
Food cost	3,000 meals × £1.83 (SP £4.50 − GP £2.67)	
	OR 3,000 meals × 0.2 kg × £9.15 per kg	5,490
Gross profit	3,000 × £2.67	8,010

(b) *Actual trading account*

		£
Sales	4,000 meals @ £4.80 per meal	19,200
Food cost	4,000 meals × 0.25 kg × £9.48 per kg	9,480
Gross profit	4,000 × £2.43	9,720

NOTE. All the figures needed for the trading accounts can be calculated from figures given in the question except the food cost. This can be calculated from the selling price and gross profit per meal, or from the quantities and price of ingredients. We are given the standard ingredient cost is £9.15 per kg, and we can calculate that the standard usage per meal is 0.2 kg per meal from the information given about ingredient usage variance. If standard usage at actual volume (4,000 meals) is 800 kg, then standard usage for one meal is 0.2 kg. Similarly actual usage at actual volume is given as 1,000 kg, so actual usage per meal must be 0.25 kg.

Change in sales mix

If total sales comprise more than one kind of item giving different rates of gross profit, then the question of sales volume will have to be divided between the overall numbers and the sales mix. Any difference in the total numbers of items will result in a sales margin quantity variance; any difference in the sales mix will cause a difference in the total gross profit, even though the total number of items sold is unchanged and each item gives the same gross profit as usual. This difference in profit is attributable to a sales margin mix variance.

In order to apportion the volume variance between the difference due to quantity and the difference due to mix it is necessary to compare:

1   the new numbers with the budgeted numbers at the same (budgeted) price, and then
2   the new total sales in their actual mix with the same sales in the budgeted mix.

These new comparisons require two new terms:

Standard sales = actual number of sales at budgeted selling price.
Revised standard sales = actual total sales at budgeted sales mix.

Sales margin volume variance = Difference in number of meals sold × budgeted gross profit per meal. This is the change in margin due to a change in numbers of items sold. It is the total of sales margin quantity variance and sales margin mix variance.

Sales margin quantity variance = Revised standard sales less budgeted sales × budgeted GP%. This gives the change in margin due to the change in total sales if the sales mix has been correctly forecast.

Sales margin mix variance = Standard sales less revised standard sales × budgeted GP%. This gives the change in margin due to the change in sales mix if the total sales has been correctly forecast.

Example

	Budget	£	*Actual*	£
Sales				
A 3,000 @ £8.00		24,000	3,200 @ £8.25	26,400
B 2,000 @ £10.00		20,000	2,200 @ £10.50	23,100
		44,000		49,500
Ingredient cost				
A 3,000 @ £3.20		9,600	3,200 @ £3.20	10,240
B 2,000 @ £4.50		9,000	2,200 @ £4.50	9,900
		18,600		20,140
Gross profit				
A 3,000 @ £4.80 (60%)		14,400	3,200 @ £5.05 (61%)	16,160
B 2,000 @ £5.50 (55%)		11,000	2,200 @ £6.00 (57%)	13,200
		25,400		29,360

In this example sales have increased from £44,000 to £49,500, partly due to increased selling prices, partly to increased sales volume. This in turn has changed in respect of both numbers of both meals, and the mix between the two.

		£
Standard sales – A 3,200 ×£8		25,600
– B 2,200 × £10		22,000
		47,600
Revised standard sales – A 24,000/44,000 × £47,600		25,964
– B 20,000/44,000 × £47,600		21,636
		47,600

Variances

Sales margin price variance

Actual price – budget price × actual number of sales

	£
A £0.25 (fav.) × 3,200	800(F)
B £0.50 (fav.) × 2,200	1,100(F)
	1,900(F)

Sales margin volume variance

Actual number of meals sold – budget number of meals sold × budget GP per meal

A 200(F) × £4.80 ·	= £ 960(F)
B 200(F) × £5.50	= £1,100
	£2,060

Sales margin quantity variance

Revised standard sales less budget sales × budget GP%

A £24,000/£44,000 × £47,600 =	£25,964	
less budget sales	£24,000	
	£ 1,964(F) × 60% =	£1,178(F)
B £20,000/£44,000 × £47,600 =	£21,636	
less budget sales	£20,000	
	£ 1,636(F) × 55% =	£ 900(F)
		2,078(F)

Sales margin mix variance

Standard sales less revised standard sales × budget GP%

A 3,200 × £8.00   £25,600   £   £
   £24/£44 × £47,600 = £25,964
                          £   364(ADV) × 60% = 218(A)
B 2,200 × £10.00   £22,000
   £20/£44 × £47,600 = £21,636
                          £   364(FAV) × 55% = 200(F)
                                                              18(A)
                   Volume variance as above   2,060(F)
Difference in total gross profit   3,960

Exercises

1 The budget and actual figures for the Fastfood Cafe are as
   follows:

	Budget	£	Actual	£
Sales 3,000 @ £3.00		9,000	4,000 @ £3.20	12,800
Ingredient cost:				
600 kg @ £6.10 kg		3,660	1,000 kg @ £6.32 kg	6,320
		5,340		6,480

You are required to calculate the following variances:

(a) Spending power variance
(b) Cover volume variance
(c) Ingredient price variance
(d) Ingredient usage variance

2 The Perspex Restaurant has prepared the following figures in
   respect of sales of one dish in the month of June:

	Budget		*Actual*	
		£		£
Sales 2,000 × £6.30		12,600	1,940 × £6.30	12,222
Cost of ingredients:				
Meat	3,520		3,550	
Other	1,520		1,560	
		5,040		5,110
Gross profit		7,560		7,112

Budget ingredients:	
Meat	500 kg @ £7.04 per kg
Other	600 kg @ £2.50 per kg
Actual ingredients:	
Meat	500 kg @ £7.10 per kg
Other	600 kg @ £2.60 per kg

You are required to

(a) calculate the variances, and
(b) reconcile the budget profit with the actual profit.

3   A restaurant's maximum possible business is ninety covers per day, and normal business includes two speciality dishes, curry and whole fish. Average occupancy is 40 per cent and one in every four customers orders a speciality dish.
   The budgeted ingredient costs and selling prices are as follows:

	Ingredient cost per dish	*Selling price per dish*
Curry	300 g meat @ £ 5.20 per kg	£4.40
Fish	400 g fish @ £ 4.40 per kg	£4.90

Cost of other ingredients in each dish is budgeted at 20p, and the actual cost is not significantly different from this.
   It was expected that sales of curry and fish would be in the ratio 5:4, but in the 4 weeks ended 28 October the actual sales were 160 curries and 110 fish.
   Because the price of meat purchases increased to £6.00 per kg from September onwards, the selling price of the curry dish was increased to £5.00 per dish for the whole of the October period. Fish prices remained unchanged, but because of the difficulty of standardising the size of fish the quantity of fish purchased differed from the budgets.
   Actual purchases were: meat 47.2 kg @ £6.00 per kg, and fish 46.2 kg @ £4.40 per kg.

You are to prepare (a) statements of budgets and actual gross profit, and (b) an analysis of the variances.

24 Inter-firm comparisons and uniform accounting

Inter-firm comparisons and uniform accounting are both attempts to help the hotel and catering industry to obtain more useful accounting information, the first from other concerns of a similar nature and the latter by standardising their own records. It will be seen that the one depends to a large extent on the other.

Inter-firm comparisons

The idea of inter-firm comparisons is that if a group of firms of similar size and type exchange information about their financial results, it will be of benefit to all those who participate. This was very successfully operated for many years in Switzerland, and by the Hotels and Motels Association of America. In the UK small groups of hotels in different parts of the country tried the scheme with growing enthusiasm as the benefit of receiving information from others became sufficiently apparent to outweigh the dread of giving information to others.

The principle of the scheme does not call for a direct exchange of financial information between hotels, but each hotel supplies certain information each month to a collecting centre, where it is processed and redistributed as anonymous group information. The information itself consists of items such as occupancy, sales mix, gross profit per cent, and labour cost per cent.

A group would consist of perhaps six to ten hotels, all having about the same number of bedrooms, and all situated in the same locality, so that comparison between them would be valid. The collecting centre is conveniently the local college, which can preserve secrecy and remain impartial. Only the centre knows details of individual hotels, which are referred to only by code numbers. The information recirculated to hotels by the centre gives the mean results of the group, which each hotel can compare with its own figures. Hotels soon discovered the benefit of knowing when their own figures were out of step with most others, and were quick to look into the reasons why.

A secondary advantage accruing out of the scheme is that hotels are encouraged to pay more attention to the accuracy of their accounting. One particular question which soon had to be settled was whether all members of the group were preparing their results in the same way. Some uniformity in accounting was essential.

Uniform accounting

Preparation of accounting information in a uniform way has long been practised by other industries, but for hotels the first step on a national scale was taken in 1969 when the Hotel and Catering Economic Development Committee published its booklet 'A Standard System of Hotel Accounting'. This was an attempt to standardise the way in which hotels dealt with their financial information, so that valid comparisons could be made.

It was realised that different firms might include items under different headings, so that any discussion on the subject of costs could be very misleading. Uniformity was to be achieved by giving every kind of income and expense a code number. It was specified which code numbers should be grouped under which group headings, and for this purpose items were grouped under three 'operated departments':

1   Rooms.
2   Food.
3   Liquor and tobacco.

Codifying every item of income and expense in this way would mean that all hotels would deal with the same items in the same way, and this could lead to worthwhile discussions throughout the industry. This first booklet was followed in 1971 by 'A Standard System of Catering Accounting', which put forward a similar proposal.

For various reasons the idea never really became universally adopted, but publishing the details of the method undoubtedly created a more general awareness of hotel and catering accounting trends.

Index